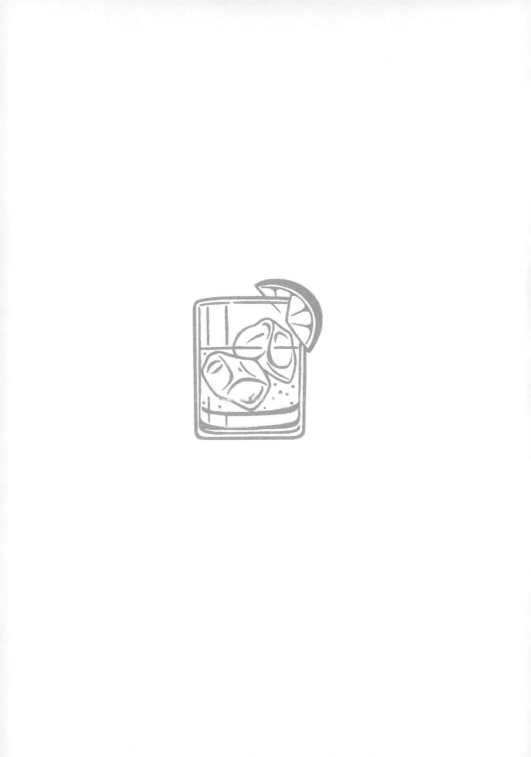

············
THE
············

GIN

DICTIONARY

An A–Z of all things gin,
from juniper berries to the G&T

DAVID T. SMITH

ILLUSTRATED BY STUART PATIENCE

MITCHELL BEAZLEY

For JPS & DWS

Contents

7   Introduction

13   A-Z

250   Index

254   Acknowledgments

256   About the author

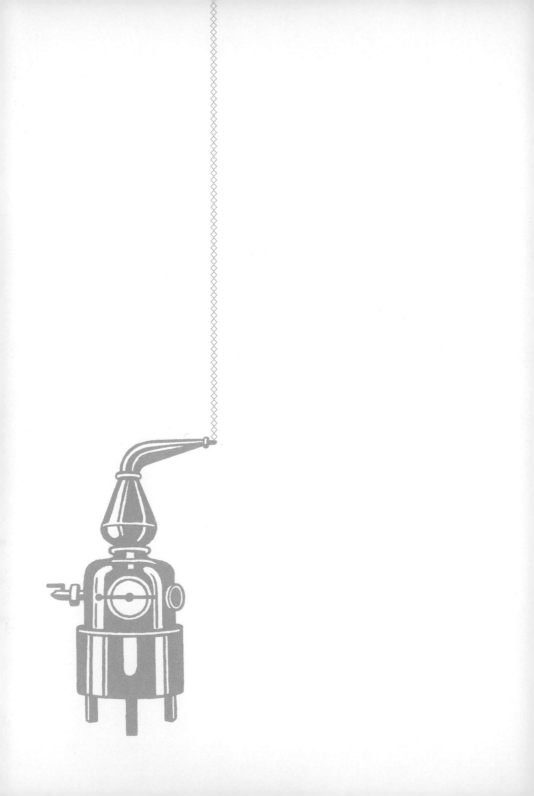

Introduction

Gin is such an exciting subject, with one foot in the past and one in the future. It has soared to giddy heights and wallowed in the gutter; perhaps the worst time of all was when, at the end of the 20th century, it was simply ignored.

The opposite can be said for gin now as it is well and truly back in vogue. Its popularity has risen and risen and something of a "gin renaissance" has spread around the world – long may the passion continue.

With such a rich tapestry of history, not to mention the range of exotic and unusual ingredients and methodologies employed in making gin, anyone trying to find out a little bit more about their favourite spirit is often left adrift in confusion and a bamboozling array of obscure definitions and terms.

This book will help to clear matters up for everyone – from those of you who are casual gin drinkers, all the way to bartenders, distillers and gin super-fans. Even the most complex of topics are presented in a concise and enjoyable way, meaning that anyone can delve a little deeper into the world of gin, and emerge with a clearer understanding of this most fascinating of drinks.

My own time in gin started in the same way as many others before me: I just really liked it. Luckily for me, my discovery of just how much I liked gin coincided with the beginning of the spirit's recent revival. This was in 2005 and I plunged headlong into the pursuit of a deeper awareness and understanding of the many varieties of the drink. In the following year, I would try my 100th gin – an achievement that I never expected to meet.

Fast forward to the present day and I have lost track of the number of new gins I have tried – likely around 1,500, including varieties from nearly 50 different countries. Nowadays, much of my time is spent sharing my passion for gin, researching new and historical production techniques and recipes, and helping distillers to perfect new gins, whether they be a small start-up or a large multinational.

Writing a book on the subject of gin gives me particular joy. For a seemingly simple, humble drink there is so much to learn about its history, varieties, techniques, craft distilleries and more that it is easy to lose oneself in the subject; uncovering unknown facts at every turn of the page. It is exciting that some of the details in this book are almost as new to me as they will be to you.

So I hope that you find this dictionary a useful tool to further your understanding of gin, whether you're a casual fan taking your first steps into understanding your favourite drink, or are already well down the road of gin expertise. Within these pages I hope to provide some small insight into just what it is that makes this wonderful spirit so special.

—David T. Smith

SEE ALSO

Navy strength gin *p167*

ABV | PRODUCTION

ABV stands for "alcohol by volume" and is a measure of alcoholic strength. ABV is expressed as a percentage and refers to the percentage of a liquid that is alcohol. Water has an alcoholic strength of 0% ABV, while pure alcohol is 100% ABV. The minimum strength of gin within the European Union (EU) is 37.5% ABV and in the USA it is 40.0% ABV. When alcohol is produced in a still, it is typically around 86% ABV. It needs to be reduced in alcoholic strength before bottling, a process known as proofing. When water is added to alcohol, an exothermic reaction happens and heat is released. In the US, a proof system is used to express the alcoholic strength of spirits, although the use of the proof system is voluntary and all bottles must also state the % ABV. US proof is simply twice the ABV, so 40.0% ABV is equivalent to 80° US proof. It should be noted that US proof is not the same as British proof, the system that predates the widescale use of ABV. For example, 100° British proof is equivalent to 57.15% ABV (*see* page 167, Navy strength gin). British proof is the equivalent of 1.75 times the ABV, so 40.0% ABV is 70° British proof.

SEE ALSO

Negroni *p168*
Red vermouth *p191*
Sipping gin *p207*
Yellow gin *p243*

Aged gin | GIN STYLE

Gin that has been matured in or with wood, using either a barrel, wood chips or staves. There are two main types of aged gin: yellow gin, which is lightly influenced by wood, and sipping gin, a more modern and popular style. Traditionally, maturation involves the storing of gin in barrels, which can be made from new oak, or can have been already used (for example ex-Bourbon barrels, which add a spicy sweetness). They may also have had some sort of additional finish, for example using a wine such as sherry, port or vermouth, which adds fruity complexity. The advantage of using barrels over other methods of maturation is that they already exist and they also allow the gin to breathe and lightly oxidize as it matures, an important part of maturation for some experts.

The advantage of using staves or chips is that there are more varieties available, including pine, mahogany or pecan, some of which would not be suitable for making into barrels, either because it would be too expensive, suitable wood is unavailable, or the wood is too porous to hold gin. Most gin drinkers and connoisseurs take a balanced approach to maturation, valuing each form for its relative merits.

SEE ALSO

Bitter almond *p25*
Botanicals *p39*

Almond *PRUNUS DULCIS VAR. DULCIS* | BOTANICAL

Native to the Mediterranean, Middle East, North America and northern India, the almond tree produces a green and fleshy plum-like fruit. This contains a shell which, in turn, contains the teardrop-shaped nut commonly referred to as an almond. Today, almond production is dominated by growers in California, USA, with other significant cultivation taking place in Spain and

A

Italy. Almond trees are exceptionally thirsty; it typically takes 4 litres (7 pints) of water to produce a single nut. In distilling, almond is used as a botanical to add dryness and mouthfeel to a gin. Beefeater is a well-known example of a gin that is flavoured with almond.

Alpine gin | GIN STYLE

A style of gin popular in countries with close proximity to the Alps mountain range, such as Germany, Austria and Switzerland. The style is characterized by strong pine and juniper notes, woody herbaceous flavours and a touch of florality. In comparison to other gins, citrus flavours are generally lighter and more reserved. Alpine gin was probably inspired by the history of making herbal spirits and liqueurs in the region. While the style is most closely associated with the Alpine region, the same flavour profile is also popular with many gin makers from the Nordic countries such as Norway, Sweden, Finland and Iceland. Gins in this style have a strong flavour profile and work well with other strong ingredients, such as the Campari and red vermouth in an intense Negroni cocktail.

Anethole | CHEMICAL COMPOUND

Also known as anise camphor, anethole is an organic compound and terpenoid which is fragrant and powerful in flavour and found in many of the botanicals used to flavour gin. It also has a sweetness more than ten times that of sugar. Anethole is abundant in nature and is found in anise and fennel, where it plays a major part in their flavour and aromatic character. It is also found in licorice, star anise, anise myrtle, tarragon, basil and cicely. The compound is

SEE ALSO
Campari *p45*
Herbal *p128*
Hernö *p128*
Negroni *p168*
Red vermouth *p191*

SEE ALSO
Licorice root *p147*
Louching *p153*
Myrtle *p164*
Star anise *p212*

highly soluble in alcohol, but only very slightly soluble in water. These characteristics are responsible for the louching of absinthe, ouzo, pastis and, in some cases, gin.

SEE ALSO

Botanical recipe *p36*
Botanicals *p39*
Dry vermouth *p80*
Fixatives *p84*
Green Chartreuse *p125*
Red vermouth *p191*

Angelica root *ANGELICA ARCHANGELICA* | BOTANICAL

The third most prolific botanical to be used in gin, angelica root is also known as wild celery or Norwegian angelica. Like many other botanicals, it is part of the Apiaceae (carrot) family. It is native to Nordic countries and western Russia. Angelica is cultivated in Germany, France and Belgium, although it now grows wild in other cool climates such as the UK, Scandinavia and parts of the USA. Angelica root is dried and then roughly chopped or chipped before being used. In gin, angelica root adds an earthy, woody, dry note and is sometimes referred to as "the botanical that gives gin its dryness". It is also often cited as a fixative in gin, helping to marry flavours together and maintain the integrity of the spirit's flavour profile. Angelica is also used in other botanical spirits and wines such as vermouth, aquavitae, Bénédictine, absinthe and Chartreuse.

Angostura bitters | COCKTAIL INGREDIENT

An aromatic non-potable bitters used as a flavouring in cocktails. "Non-potable" refers to the fact that these are not designed to be drunk on their own, but instead used in small amounts to season drinks and accentuate the flavours of the other ingredients. The recipe for Angostura bitters was developed in the 19th century by the Surgeon-General of the Venezuelan Army, Johann Gottlieb Benjamin Siegert. Siegert was based in the town of Angostura (now Ciudad

Bolívar), hence the name of the bitters. He sold his first bitters in 1824 and started exporting them in 1830. Siegert died in 1870 and, five years later, production moved to the Port of Spain in Trinidad, where they are still made today. Angostura bitters should not be confused with bitters made from angostura bark, a medicinal plant native to South America. Siegert's bitters are not made using angostura bark, although the bark is named after the same town in Venezuela.

SEE ALSO
Crème de Violette *p71*
Glassware *p119*
Ice *p135*
Shaken/Shaking *p201*

Aviation | COCKTAIL

A cocktail thought to have been created by Hugo R Ensslin, Head Bartender at Hotel Wallick located at Broadway and 43rd Street in New York City. The original recipe called for El Bart Gin, which was a popular contemporary of Gordon's and Plymouth during the early 20th century. It was made by Wilson Distilling of Bristol, Pennsylvania, although it was made under licence from the Camberwell Distillery of London, UK. Gin is mixed with lemon juice, maraschino and Crème de Violette (which gives it a distinctive blue colour). During the mid-20th century, Crème de Violette became harder to obtain and, as a result, some recipes now omit the floral liqueur. Instead, the sweetness comes from the maraschino; this not only changes the flavour of the drink, but the colour too.

AVIATION RECIPE

50 ML / 2 FL OZ / GIN
20 ML / ⅔ FL OZ / FRESH LEMON JUICE
10 ML / ⅓ FL OZ / MARASCHINO
10 ML / ⅓ FL OZ / CRÈME DE VIOLETTE

Place all the ingredients into a cocktail shaker filled with ice, shake well and strain into a cocktail glass.

SEE ALSO
ABV *p13*
Botanical recipe *p36*
Botanicals *p39*
Honey *p131*

Base spirit | PRODUCTION

Gin is produced by redistilling a neutral alcohol with botanicals to add character to the drink. This alcohol is known as the base spirit; it forms the blank canvas for the botanical flavours and aromas to overlay. Many gin distilleries, including all of the big gin brands, use a neutral spirit purchased from a third party. This is usually made from grain, so it is known as Neutral Grain Spirit (NGS) or Grain Neutral Spirit (GNS), although spirits made from grape and molasses are also available. In Europe, the base spirit of gin has to have been distilled to 96% ABV. This removes a lot, but not all, of the character of the base spirit's raw materials. The advantage of using NGS is that it involves less capital expenditure, because a distillery does not need to buy a column still (required to distil efficiently to high ABVs) and the spirit is often more neutral in character. Some producers make their own base spirit. This is particularly common in the United States, where these producers are often referred to as "grain to glass" distillers. The benefit of "grain-to-glass" is that a distiller gains greater control, allowing them to use a base spirit that may not be readily available from a third party, such as spirit made from honey or apples.

SEE ALSO
Compounded gin *p64*
Prohibition *p183*

**TYPICAL CHARACTERS OF
BASE SPIRIT MATERIALS**

WHEAT: CLEAN AND NEUTRAL

CORN: CLEAN WITH A LIGHT SWEETNESS

BARLEY: CLEAN WITH A LIGHT, CREAMY SPICE

MALTED BARLEY: ADDS SOME BREADY NOTES

APPLE: FRESH AND CRISP WITH A LIGHT FRUITINESS

GRAPE: FLORAL AND FRUITY

MOLASSES: SMOOTH AND SILKY WITH A LIGHT SWEETNESS

HONEY: MELLOW, WITH A THICK TEXTURE AND FLORAL
     SWEETNESS

Bathtub gin | GIN STYLE

The term originates from the early days of
American Prohibition in the 1920s. It was used
to describe the illicitly produced, compounded
gin being drunk at various speakeasies in the
United States. The exact origins of the term are
uncertain, but there are two main theories. One
is that the containers used to mix the ingredients
were too large to be topped up with water from
a sink tap and so were filled from a bath tap;
the second theory is that baths, being large
containers themselves, were used to mix the
alcohol and various botanicals. The term tended
to be used in a pejorative way until 2011, when
Atom Supplies launched a product called Bathtub
Gin. This starts life as a relatively simple London
gin and is then flavoured with more botanicals
via infusion. The product has received great
critical acclaim since its launch, thus improving
the image of bathtub gin.

SEE ALSO
Bitter orange *p26*
Botanical recipe *p36*
Botanicals *p39*
Lime (Persian) *p148*

Bergamot orange *CITRUS BERGAMIA* | BOTANICAL

A hybrid of sweet lime (*Citrus limetta*) and bitter
orange (*Citrus* x *aurantium*), which is used to
flavour some gins. The fruit is similar in size
to a bitter orange, but has a green peel when
ripe. Bergamot orange is also used to make

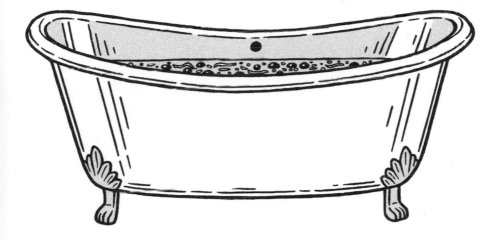

marmalade and to flavour confectionery such as Turkish delight. The essential oil extracted from the peel of the fruit is notably used in Earl Grey tea, where it provides the tea's distinctive aromatic and citrus character. In 2016, the Torino Distillery started producing a bergamot-flavoured liqueur named Italicus Rosolio di Bergamotto. In gin production, the peels of bergamot are used for their aromatic and floral citrus notes as well their slight bitterness. They can be used in either dried or fresh form. Gins made using bergamot orange peel as a botanical include Fifty Eight Gin and Boxer Gin, both made in London. Fifty Eight Gin is made from the company's own bergamot peel, which is dried in house.

SEE ALSO

Almond *p15*

Bombay Spirits Company *p33*

Botanical recipe *p36*

Botanicals *p39*

Bitter almond

PRUNUS DULCIS VAR. AMARA | BOTANICAL

Some varieties of almond tree produce nuts that are smaller and more bitter than those of the sweet almond (*Prunus dulcis* var. *dulcis*). These are native to Asia and the Middle East and are known as "bitter almonds". The term is also sometimes used to describe the kernels of apricots (*Prunus armeniaca*), peaches (*Prunus persica*) and plums (*Prunus domestica*). The essential oil of bitter almonds is largely benzaldehyde. They were once used more frequently in food and drink (including gin), but concerns over the levels of hydrogen cyanide yielded from compounds within the seeds have severely reduced their use and availability. Bitter almonds are typically sourced from the USA or Spain. Gins that use bitter almonds as a botanical include Beefeater, Bombay Dry Gin and Oxley.

SEE ALSO

Garnishes *p93*
Ice *p135*
Quinine *p185*
Sloe gin *p208*
Soda water *p208*
Tonic water *p226*

Bitter lemon | COCKTAIL INGREDIENT

Also known as lemon tonic, this soft drink is a variation on tonic water and is flavoured with lemon, lime, citric acid and quinine. Early versions of this drink were simply a mixture of Schweppes Soda Water and lime juice; the earliest recorded reference to this is 1834. Bitter lemon was officially launched by Schweppes on 1 May 1957, along with a Bitter Orange drink. Previously, the British firm Lyons had released a tonic water mixed with lemon juice. Bitter lemon is commonly drunk on its own as a soft drink, although the increased tartness over regular tonic water also makes it a good partner for sweeter spirits and liqueurs such as sloe gin. The Long Pedlar is a combination of sloe gin, bitter lemon and ice. Both the name and drink were created by James Hawker and Co Ltd in Plymouth for use with their Hawkers Pedlar Sloe Gin. The drink was designed as a way to enjoy sloe gin, typically consumed in the colder months, during warm weather too.

THE LONG PEDLAR RECIPE

50ML / 2FL OZ / SLOE GIN
150ML / 5FL OZ / BITTER LEMON
LEMON AND LIME, TO GARNISH

Fill a glass with ice and pour over the sloe gin and bitter lemon. Garnish "Evans style" with lemon and lime (see page 94).

Bitter orange *CITRUS X AURANTIUM* | BOTANICAL

Also known as the Seville or sour orange, this fruit features as a flavouring in many gins. Like its cousin the sweet orange, this citrus fruit is a hybrid of the pomelo and the mandarin. It originates in Southeast Asia and was introduced to Spain in the 10th century. Varieties of the

SEE ALSO

Botanical recipe *p36*
Botanicals *p39*
Cardamom *p49*
Cassia bark *p50*
Citrus *p58*
Gordon's *p120*
Limonene *p148*
Linalool *p150*
Sweet orange *p216*

tree now grow in many countries across the world. The peel of the bitter orange has a strong aroma and flavour, and a distinctive, zesty bitterness. It is often used in the production of marmalade. In drinks, bitter orange is used to flavour a wide variety of spirits and liqueurs, and is a key ingredient in orange bitters. The chemical components of bitter orange peel include limonene, myrcene and linalool. When used as a gin botanical, it adds a zestiness similar to sweet orange, but with deeper, darker notes and a definite bitterness. It pairs well with other sweeter botanicals such as cassia and cardamom. Due to its intensity, bitter orange should be used sparingly in gin. The peels can be used fresh, but it is more common for them to be used in a dried state. Examples of gins that use bitter orange as a botanical include Gordon's, Hayman's London Dry Gin, City of London Dry Gin and Sipsmith.

Black peppercorn *PIPER NIGRUM* | BOTANICAL

SEE ALSO
Bombay Spirits Company *p33*
Botanical recipe *p36*
Botanicals *p39*
Cubeb berries *p73*
Grains of paradise *p123*
Hernö *p128*
Pink peppercorn *p178*

The fruit of a flowering vine, native to India, belonging to the Piperaceae family and used as a botanical in gin production. Black peppercorns are made when the unripe fruits are cooked and dried; green peppercorns are the unripe dried fruits; and white peppercorns are the dried ripe fruits. All peppercorns, especially the black variety, are used for the seasoning and flavouring of food throughout the world. In the Western world, black pepper sits alongside salt to form the traditional table cruet set. The signature peppery flavour of the dried fruit comes from the chemical piperine. Vietnam is the number one producer of pepper, accounting for more than one-third of the world's supply. Black peppercorns are most commonly used in gin production and are most often utilized in their whole state. Like cubeb berries and grains of paradise, their addition to a gin's botanical recipe tends to lengthen the finish and add a bright spiciness and peppery warmth to the flavour profile. Notable gins containing black pepper include Bombay Sapphire East and most of the gins in the Hernö range.

SEE ALSO

Botanical recipe *p36*
Botanicals *p39*
London gin *p151*
Rotovap *p194*
Vacuum distillation *p233*

Blended gin | GIN STYLE

A gin made by distilling each botanical individually in separate distillation runs and then blending the distillates together in the desired proportions to produce the final gin. While it is most common for each botanical to be distilled separately, some distillers group them together, for example distilling a variety of citrus peels or flowers together. Advocates of blended gin claim that the method helps to maintain greater balance and consistency than traditional methods of gin production. In addition, distilling the botanicals separately allows distillers greater control over the rate of extraction of the flavours and aromas. They can customize the maceration time, temperature, alcoholic strength of the charge and how aggressively the still is run for each botanical or set of botanicals. For example, for fresh leaves or flowers, the still can be run at a lower temperature to avoid overcooking the botanicals, which can cause the extraction of stewed flavours. There is a question as to whether or not a blended gin can be considered London gin according to EU regulations. The problem arises because, at the time that the regulations were finalized in 2007, no distiller was using this method. Examples of blended gins include Sacred, Sloane's and Gin Mare.

SEE ALSO

Bergamot orange *p22*
Black peppercorn *p29*
Botanical recipe *p36*
Botanicals *p39*
Cubeb berries *p73*
Grains of paradise *p123*
Greenall's *p126*
Lemongrass *p144*
London gin *p151*
Vapour distillation *p234*

Bombay Spirits Company | BRAND

The history of the Bombay Gin brand dates back to 1957, when New York lawyer, Allan Subin, decided to launch a new gin brand in the United States. He wanted it to be the embodiment of Englishness and so went to Greenall's Distillery and asked them to make a vapour-infused, grain-based gin based on their recipe from 1761. The gin was launched as Bombay Dry Gin in 1960 and, by 1964, was selling 10,000 cases a year. This increased to 100,000 cases by 1970. In 1980, the company was sold to International Distillers and Vintners.

By the late 1970s, tastes had moved away from gin and towards vodka. This continued in the 1980s, with the launch of Absolut Vodka. Bombay reacted to this by launching Bombay Sapphire, named after the Star of Bombay, the blue sapphire that also inspired their bottle's iconic colour. With two new exotic botanicals – cubeb berries and grains of paradise – Bombay Sapphire was one of the first truly luxury gins. The smooth flavour produced by the gin's vapour distillation also made it accessible to new converts to gin.

In 1997, the brand was sold by Diageo to Bacardi. In 2011, Bombay Spirits launched Bombay Sapphire East for the American market. This gin was made with additional botanicals such as lemongrass and black peppercorn. The year 2014 saw the short-lived release of an aged gin, Bombay Amber, which was discontinued in the same year. Also that year, the company opened the Bombay Sapphire Distillery at Laverstoke Mill in Hampshire in the UK (left). A year later, the distillery released Star of Bombay, a gin that added ambrette seeds and bergamot to their traditional botanical recipe; this gin was

SEE ALSO

Aged gin *p15*

Gin house *p107*

London gin *p151*

Martini *p159*

Sipping gin *p207*

Yellow gin *p243*

awarded the London Dry Gin Trophy at the 2016 International Wine and Spirits Competition.

Booth's | BRAND

A gin brand and gin house founded around 1740 by John Booth, father of Sir Felix Booth. The brand has a distinctive red lion on its labels. The company was listed as Philip Booth & Company Distillers of Clerkenwell in a 1778 directory. It was owned by the family until 1896, when it became a limited company. It is now owned by Diageo. In the 1920s and 1930s, Booth's expanded, buying out Boord's Gin. They made two London dry gins under the Booth's label: Booth's Finest (or House of Lords) and Booth's High and Dry.

According to legend, Booth's House of Lords Gin came about when some finished gin, stored in a barrel, had been forgotten about and, when tasted, was found to have a mellow flavour from the wood. In response, Booth's started to deliberately age one of their dry gins for a period of a few weeks. For most of its life, Booth's gin was aged in ex-sherry barrels but, in the 1980s, this changed to Burgundy barrels. By the early 1990s, Booth's Finest had been discontinued. Advertising for the brand is readily available, showing the golden colour and describing it as "the essential ingredient of a Perfect Martini". By the 1990s, Booth's High and Dry Gin was only for sale in the United States and was sold in plastic bottles as a budget gin. In 2016, Booth's resurrected their House of Lords Gin as a premium offering, adopting an ornate glass bottle and a more intensely matured gin style, with the spirit being aged in ex-sherry casks.

SEE ALSO
Base spirit *p21*
Juniper (common) *p137*

Borovička | GIN STYLE

A juniper spirit native to Slovakia, the Czech Republic and Hungary. It is made by steeping fermented juniper berries in a base spirit before distilling it in a similar way to gin. Because of the fermentation of the berries, some of the sugar from the juniper turns to alcohol; this is then distilled along with the base spirit, which is generally grain. This gives borovička a much stronger, resinous juniper flavour than more typical gins. The origins of borovička go back to the 16th century, when juniper berries were used to help cover up the impurities in poor-quality vodka. Today, some types of borovička are sold with a juniper berry or two in the bottle, which turns the liquid a pale golden colour. In addition, some of the larger brands also sell borovička flavoured with lime, pink grapefruit, red juniper or local mountain flowers. Borovička is usually drunk chilled and neat, often in a celebratory fashion similar to vodka.

SEE ALSO
ABV *p13*
Base spirit *p21*
Botanicals *p39*
Limonene *p148*
London cut *p151*
Pot distillation *p182*
Rectification *p187*

Botanical cuts | PRODUCTION

During a distillation run, when the distillate is being created from a combination of base spirit and botanicals, it is necessary to disregard the early and latter parts of the run, only keeping the middle part to produce the gin. This is known as "taking cuts" or "taking botanical cuts". A similar process is also common when distilling whisky, rum or brandy because it is necessary to remove poisonous methanol from the final product. Taking cuts in gin production is not necessary to produce a safe product, but is used instead to improve the quality and character of the gin. The first cuts discarded are known as "heads" or "foreshots", while those discarded from the end of the run are known as the "tails" or "feints". The middle part of the run, which is pure and kept for proofing and bottling, is known as the "hearts".

The most volatile essential oils in gin botanicals, such as limonene, come off the still at the beginning of the distillation run. In high concentrations, these can leave the final gin hot, sour and slightly bitter. Heads cuts are typically around 89–93% ABV. Toward the end of the run, heavier, green and slightly funky botanical notes come over. If too many of these are included in the gin, it makes the spirit harsh and adds a funky, slightly dirty character. They can also cause drinkers to experience an effect similar to heartburn after drinking. If a gin is referred to as "Distiller's cut", more of the heads and tails have been discarded to create an even purer and cleaner gin. Such gins are often also bottled at a higher ABV.

Botanical recipe | PRODUCTION

A botanical recipe defines the character of each individual gin, describing not only the selection of botanicals used to make the gin, but the quantities used. It may also contain finer details on how the botanicals are processed, for example whether they are milled or crushed before use and whether they are used fresh or dry, powdered or whole. A botanical recipe will detail which botanicals, if any, need to be macerated or steeped in alcohol (either hot or cold), for what length of time and the alcoholic strength of the spirit they are macerated in. The following (see page 39) is an example of a recipe for 10 litres (17½ pints) of base spirit at 50% ABV.

SEE ALSO
Angelica root *p19*
Base spirit *p21*
Bitter orange *p26*
Black peppercorn *p29*
Botanicals *p39*
Coriander seed *p68*
Ginger *p114*
Juniper (common) *p137*
Lavender *p143*
Maceration *p155*
Sweet orange *p216*

60G / 2OZ / JUNIPER BERRIES
60G / 2OZ / CORIANDER SEED
10G / ⅓OZ / ANGELICA ROOT
6G / ⅕OZ / DRIED GINGER ROOT
3G / ¹⁄₁₀OZ / DRIED ORANGE PEEL
3G / ¹⁄₁₀OZ / BLACK PEPPERCORNS
2.5G / ¹⁄₁₂OZ / DRIED LAVENDER

Botanicals | PRODUCTION

SEE ALSO
Almond p15
Bergamot orange p22
Bitter orange p26
Botanical recipe p36
Caraway p46
Cassia bark p50
Cinnamon p57
Coriander seed p68
Juniper (common) p137
Juniper (other species) p138
Lemon p143
Lemongrass p144
Lime (Persian) p148
Rosemary p192
Sweet orange p216

The raw materials, combined to form a botanical recipe, that give a gin its flavour and aroma. With very few exceptions, botanicals are naturally occurring ingredients and include juniper (essential for any gin); roots such as angelica and ginger; the peel of citrus fruits including lemon, lime, orange and bergamot; tree barks such as cinnamon and cassia; seeds including fennel, coriander or caraway; leaves such as basil, rosemary and bay; and a host of other plant material including other fruits, lemongrass and almonds. Botanicals typically come in either dried or fresh forms. Fresh botanicals will usually have a brighter flavour, but are more susceptible to damage, especially when they are heated. Dried botanicals tend to be more consistent and stand up better to the heat of distillation, but the variety commercially available may be more limited.

Bramble | COCKTAIL

SEE ALSO
Garnishes p93
Glassware p119
Ice p135

A gin cocktail invented by Dick Bradsell in 1984 at Fred's Club in Soho, London, made from gin, lemon juice, sugar syrup and Crème de Mûre. The drink can trace its ancestry back to 1862 in the form of the Gin Fix from Jerry Thomas' cocktail guide, *How to Mix Drinks*, which contained a mixture of gin, sugar, lemon and water. In the 1960s, a cocktail called the Canadian Blackberry Fix was published in various books. This recipe combined blackberries with Canadian whiskey instead of gin. The Bramble has a great balance between sweet and sour flavours; the sourness comes from the lemon juice and the sweetness from the sugar syrup and Crème de Mûre. Crème de Mûre is a particularly sweet liqueur flavoured with blackberries, which grow on a rough, prickly shrub, sometimes known as "brambles", hence the cocktail's name. Sometimes, Crème de Mûre is replaced by Chambord, a black raspberry-flavoured liqueur. The resulting cocktail is not a true Bramble, however, as the flavour of the liqueur is significantly different and makes the drink much sweeter. The Bramble can be garnished with fresh berries and lemon.

THE BRAMBLE RECIPE

25ML / ¾FL OZ / GIN
25ML / ¾FL OZ / FRESH LEMON JUICE
25ML / ¾FL OZ / SIMPLE SUGAR SYRUP
20ML / ⅔FL OZ / CRÈME DE MÛRE

Fill a glass with crushed ice, add the first three ingredients and stir. Drizzle over the Crème de Mûre.

British juniper *JUNIPERUS COMMUNIS* | BOTANICAL

SEE ALSO
Juniper (common) *p137*
Terroir *p221*

British juniper refers to any plant of *Juniperus communis* that is harvested from Great Britain and used in gin production. *Juniperus communis* is one of only three conifers native to the UK. Juniper bushes were once plentiful, but even by 1802, a distiller's manual noted that they were often sourced from Germany. At that time, Germany was still part of the Holy Roman Empire, whose territories included northern Italy, an area that is still known for growing juniper today. Imported juniper was often chosen because British bushes were not large

enough. Despite this, it was still an accepted practice to use British juniper, although the author of the manual cautions that they should be fully ripe and need to be dried thoroughly before packing for storage in sealed barrels.

The number of juniper bushes in the United Kingdom has further declined due to the clearance of land for agriculture. This was especially true during the Second World War, when the domestic food supply was severely threatened. Today, juniper bushes are further threatened by the fungus *Phytophthora austrocedrae*. However, a number of gins still use British juniper. Crossbill Gin of Scotland contains just two botanicals: British juniper and rosehips harvested from the Cairngorm Mountains. Hepple Gin uses locally sourced juniper berries in their green, unripe state, along with imported ripe berries. And Beckett's Gin uses juniper collected from Box Hill in Surrey.

Burrough's | BRAND

SEE ALSO
Gin house *p107*
London gin *p151*
Navy strength gin *p167*
Old Tom gin *p171*

An historic gin house founded by chemist James Burrough (1835–1876). Burrough bought his first distillery in Chelsea, London, in 1862 and started to produce gin the following year. By 1876, the distillery was producing multiple brands of gin, including James Burrough London Dry and some Old Tom gins. Burrough decided to name his flagship gin Beefeater, rather than giving it the family name. This distinguished it from those of the other gin houses of the time. After Burrough died in 1876, the family purchased premises nearby in Lambeth, which would become Cale Distillery. They stayed in this location until 1958, during which time they started exporting to the United States. The distillery moved once more to a site in Kennington, where it still stands and produces Beefeater Gin to this day. In 2005, Beefeater was acquired by Pernod-Ricard and in 2014 they opened a visitor centre.

In 1951, Neville Hayman, who married James Burrough's granddaughter Marjorie, had started working at Burrough's; their son, Christopher Hayman, joined the family business in 1969. After the Burrough family sold the company to Whitbread in 1987, the Haymans bought back the James Burrough Fine Alcohols Division and renamed it Hayman Distillers; they now produce a range of gins including Hayman's London Dry Gin and Hayman's Royal Dock Navy Strength Gin.

Bush gin | GIN STYLE

SEE ALSO
Botanicals p39
Flavour profiles p87
Myrtle p164
Terroir p221

Originating in Australia, this style of gin is also known as Aussie gin. Bush gin first emerged as a style in the second decade of the 21st century, inspired by the unique wildlife of Australia, where 80 percent of the local floral and fauna is endemic: not only native to the country, but not found anywhere else in the world. Influenced by the Bush Food Movement's use of native plants for cooking, Australian distillers wanted to embrace the use of local botanicals. Bush gin has a bold and flavoursome character, often accompanied by leafy-citrus or spicy-menthol flavour profiles. Some gins utilize local wine for their base spirit and almost all of the gins are flavoured via distillation, then infusion. Popular botanicals include lemon myrtle, cinnamon myrtle, bush tomato, finger limes, Tasmanian pepperberry and wattle seeds.

SEE ALSO
Botanical recipe *p36*
Botanicals *p39*

Calamus *ACORUS CALAMUS* | BOTANICAL

Native to India, this once-popular gin botanical has fallen out of favour, largely due to its being removed from the United States' "generally recognized as safe list" in 1968. This was following an experiment where rats were exposed to large doses of beta-asarone for a prolonged period of time, resulting in carcinogenic effects. Although it was not clear whether the observed effects were relevant to humans, calamus products were banned as they contain beta-asarone. Calamus remains legal in most other countries and has various culinary uses. The rhizome, an underground root structure, is used as a botanical in vermouth, liqueurs, absinthes and some gins. The candied version of the rhizome is known in Europe as "German ginger". Calamus has also been used in traditional Chinese and Indian medicine for many years, where it is said to aid digestion and treat anxiety. Gins made using calamus include Colonsay Gin, Silverback Gin and Stovell's Gin.

SEE ALSO
Negroni *p168*
Red vermouth *p191*

Campari | COCKTAIL INGREDIENT

Originally from Italy, Campari is a bright crimson-red, bittersweet liqueur. It was created in 1860 by Gaspare Campari in Novara, Italy, and is made with a host of botanicals, including chinotto and cascarilla, although the rest of the ingredients remain a secret. Until 2006, the red colour came from carmine, which is derived from the powdered bodies of scale or cochineal insects. Campari's main connection to gin is as one of the three key ingredients in a Negroni cocktail. It is also used in other drinks, such as the Americano and the Boulevardier (a mix of Bourbon, Campari and red vermouth).

Caraway *CARUM CARVI* | BOTANICAL

SEE ALSO
Botanical recipe *p36*
Botanicals *p39*
Hendrick's *p127*
Limonene *p148*

A member of the Apiaceae (carrot) family, caraway produces seeds that are commonly used as a spice and are sometimes referred to as meridian fennel. Although we call them seeds, the spice is actually the split halves of the dried fruit of the plant. It is native to southern Europe and has had medicinal and culinary uses for more than two thousand years. Caraway has a lightly bitter, nutty taste with a slight sharpness and a touch of aromatic sweetness. The main component of the essential oil contained within the seeds is carvone, although they also contain limonene. In the production of drinks, caraway is commonly used as a botanical to flavour a range of spirits, including kümmel and aquavit. In gin, caraway is used sparingly to add a leafy spice complexity and a touch of sweetness, as well as adding body to the spirit's finish. Gins made using caraway as a botanical include St George Botanivore and St George Dry Rye Gins from California, Hendrick's Gin and Aviation.

Cardamom *ELETTARIA CARDAMOMUM, AMOMUM SUBULATUM* | BOTANICAL

SEE ALSO
Botanical recipe *p36*
Botanicals *p39*
Ginger *p114*
Navy strength gin *p167*
Plymouth Gin *p178*

There are two main types of cardamom: green (*Elettaria cardamomum*) and black (*Amomum*

subulatum). Also known as true cardamom, green cardamom is a member of the ginger family. It is native to southern India and Sri Lanka, although it is now grown in other tropical regions. The seed pods of the plant are light green and paper-like in texture. They contain small, black seeds. The pod itself has little aroma or flavour but the seeds are intensely flavoured and perfumed with floral hints of ginger and spice. During distillation, it is possible to extract the essential oils from within the pods by placing them in the still intact; however, some distillers lightly crack open the pods first. Green cardamom adds a bold spiciness, along with a little sweetness and notes of cassia and ginger. It can easily overpower other botanicals, so is used sparingly. Green cardamom is the third most expensive spice in the world, after saffron and vanilla. Examples of gins made using green cardamom are Sacred Cardamom Gin, Plymouth Gin and Bathtub Navy Strength Gin. The black cardamom plant is a larger relative of green cardamom. The pods are typically dried over open flames, giving them a touch of smokiness. When distilled as a botanical in gin, it adds an aromatic, oily-spiced flavour and deep, menthol pepper notes. Gins made using black cardamom include Dodd's Gin and Bombay Amber.

Carterhead still | PRODUCTION

A type of still designed and first manufactured in the late 19th century by the Carter brothers, who had previously worked for Aeneas Coffey, the pioneer of continuous distillation. The still consists of a round pot, with a typical capacity of around 3,000 litres (660 gallons), which contains the charge of spirit. On top of this is the "Carter head", a rectifying column. A pipe

SEE ALSO
ABV *p13*
Bombay Spirits Company *p33*
Botanicals *p39*
Charge *p54*
Hendrick's *p127*
Pot distillation *p182*
Rectification *p187*

from the top of the column runs up to the base
of a chamber containing a botanical basket,
which allows alcohol vapour to pass among the
botanicals inside and extract their essential oils.
A pipe from the top of this chamber leads to the
condenser. In a traditional Carterhead, it is not
easy to make gin by adding botanicals directly to
the pot, because draining and cleaning would be
difficult, so all of the gin's botanicals are placed
in the botanical basket. The still was originally
designed to rectify spirit produced on the
Coffey still, to make it cleaner and more suitable
for vodka or gin production. The rectifying
column purifies the spirit and increases its ABV.
This makes the extraction of the botanicals'
aromas and flavours easier and more efficient.
Carterhead stills are used by Rekya Distillery,
Hendrick's and Bombay Sapphire, although
following an adjustment in 2014, the original
Carterhead stills of Bombay Sapphire at
Laverstoke Mill are now known as Dakin stills.

Cassia bark *CINNAMOMUM CASSIA* | BOTANICAL

The dried bark of an evergreen tree native to
southern China. It is a spice closely related
to cinnamon and is often mistaken for true
cinnamon (*Cinnamomum verum*). It is also
known as Chinese cassia. Cassia bark has an oily
sweetness and pungent, woody, spiced flavour,
as well as a little warmth. The dried bark is
typically less tightly wound than the quills of
true cinnamon and is most commonly available
in chipped or powdered forms. It is frequently
used in confectionary such as boiled sweets
and Big Red chewing gum, as well as pastries and
desserts. In alcoholic beverages, it is often used
as an additional flavour to modify a base spirit.
This is illustrated by the great range of whiskies

SEE ALSO
Bombay Spirits Company *p33*
Botanical recipe *p36*
Botanicals *p39*
Cinnamon *p57*
Hendrick's *p127*
Martin Miller's *p156*

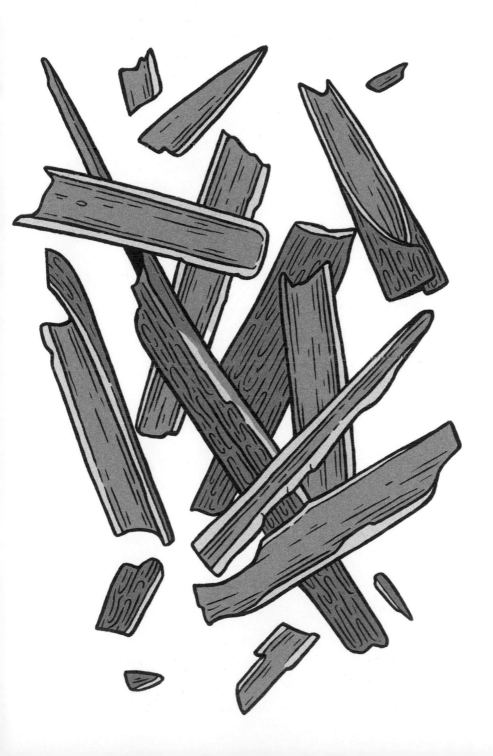

that are flavoured with cassia, which is prized
for both its sweetness and its heat. Like true
cinnamon, the characteristic flavour and aroma
of cassia bark is a result of its main chemical
component cinnamaldehyde. In gin, cassia
bark adds a little botanical sweetness, as well
as some spice and complexity. It is typically used
in chipped form, although it is possible to use it in
larger bark pieces or as a powder. Given its
similarity to true cinnamon, it is rare but not
unknown for both to be used in the same gin
recipe. Many gins are made using cassia bark
as a botanical, including Bombay Dry, Bombay
Sapphire, Bombay Sapphire East, Broker's Gin,
Martin Miller's Gin and Shortcross Gin.

Chamomile *CHAMAEMELUM NOBILE* | BOTANICAL

SEE ALSO
Botanical recipe *p36*
Botanicals *p39*
Pinene *p177*
Tanqueray *p219*

A daisy-like flower used as a botanical in gin
production, commonly known as Roman or
English chamomile. The name comes from the
Greek for "earth apple", which was inspired by
the flower's apple-like scent. Chamomile flowers
are typically used dried, either as whole flowers
or lightly ground. The scent is used in various
perfumes, toiletries and cosmetics. Chamomile
is also used to make both hot and iced teas and
has uses in traditional medicine, in particular
as an aid to sleep and relaxation. The flavours of
chamomile are soluble in both water and alcohol.
The chemical components of the essential oil in
chamomile include alpha-pinene, beta-pinene,
camphene, myrcene and sabinene. Chamomile
has a soft, slightly sweet, hay-like aroma with a
touch of red apple and light vanilla. In gin, it adds
subtle floral notes and helps to provide a balance
to citrus flavours. Gins made using chamomile
include Bloom and Tanqueray No. Ten.

SEE ALSO
ABV *p13*
Botanicals *p39*
Carterhead still *p50*
Pot distillation *p182*

Charge | PRODUCTION

The charge refers to the alcohol that is placed into the main body, or pot, boiler or kettle, of a still. For pot distillation this will include the botanicals, but for vapour distillation it will not (instead, they will be placed in the vapour or botanical basket). Alternatively, distillers may use a combination of the two methods, with botanicals forming part of the charge and also being placed in the botanical basket. The alcoholic strength of the charge has an important impact on the resulting flavour of the gin. For pot distillation, this is usually 35–60% ABV. If delicate botanicals are used and their essential oils are soluble in water, a charge with a lower ABV is recommended as the oils can still be extracted without damaging the structure of the botanicals. During vapour distillation, especially in a hybrid pot-column or Carterhead still, a higher ABV can be used; some distilleries using this method use a charge of 86% ABV.

SEE ALSO
Botanical recipe *p36*
Botanicals *p39*
Coriander seed *p68*

Cilantro *CORIANDRUM SATIVUM* | BOTANICAL

Coriander, often known as cilantro, is the green stalks and leaves from the coriander plant and is commonly used as a botanical in gin production. Cilantro is often used in cuisine, especially in India where it is cooked in curries and other dishes, and in the Caribbean and Latin America. It is also sometimes used as a garnish in a similar way to parsley. Cilantro is a very polarizing flavour, with some people thoroughly enjoying it and others being overly sensitive to it, often finding it to taste of soap. An individual's response to cilantro is likely, in part, to be due to the sensitivity of their taste buds; it tends to

be particularly unpopular with supertasters. In gin, cilantro can add a citrus leafiness. However it is important that it is used sparingly, as too much can give the spirit an unpleasant, soapy bitterness. Gins that feature cilantro include St George Spirits' Botanivore Gin.

Cinnamon *CINNAMOMUM VERUM* | BOTANICAL

SEE ALSO
Botanical recipe *p36*
Botanicals *p39*
Cassia bark *p50*
Limonene *p148*
Linalool *p150*
Navy strength gin *p167*

Also known as true or Ceylon cinnamon, this spice is not to be confused with the cheaper cassia bark (*Cinnamomum cassia*), although cassia is often sold as "cinnamon", especially in the United States. This confusion is especially likely when buying cinnamon in powdered form as it is more difficult to tell the two apart. Both are used as botanicals to flavour gin. True cinnamon is sourced from the inner bark of a small evergreen tree and, in its whole form, is sold as dried quills or cinnamon sticks that are tightly curled in on themselves. True cinnamon is native to Sri Lanka, which was formerly known as Ceylon, hence the common name. True cinnamon is also grown in the islands of the Seychelles and Madagascar. The spice's flavour is more subtle and elegant than that of cassia, and is somewhat drier and woodier. It is also significantly more expensive. The essential oil of cinnamon can be prepared by pummelling the bark, macerating it in seawater and then distilling the resulting mixture. True cinnamon contains the chemical compounds cinnamaldehyde, linalool, eugenol and limonene. In addition to its use as a gin botanical, cinnamon is also used to flavour other alcoholic drinks such as vodka and whisky, to produce flavoured whisky or whisky liqueur. Gins that use cinnamon as a botanical include Bathtub Gin, Blackwater No. 5 Gin and Perry's Tot Navy Strength Gin.

SEE ALSO

Bitter orange *p26*

Classic/Juniper-forward *p58*

Flavour profiles *p87*

Floral *p87*

Gin Tonica *p113*

Grapefruit *p124*

Herbal *p128*

Lemon *p143*

Lemongrass *p144*

Lime (Persian) *p148*

Spicy *p212*

Sweet orange *p216*

Tanqueray *p219*

Citrus | FLAVOUR PROFILE

A popular flavour profile for gins, where the flavours of citrus peels – for example lemon, lime, a variety of grapefruit and bitter or sweet orange – play a prominent role. Gins often focus on these notes because of the lively and refreshing quality of citrus flavours. Because of these qualities, citrus gins often work well in long drinks such as the Gin Tonica or Tom Collins. Le Tribute Gin from Spain is made using six varieties of citrus peel: lemon, lime, orange, grapefruit, kumquat and tangerine, all in addition to lemongrass, which adds further citrus notes. Other examples of citrus gins include Bluecoat, Hunters and Tanqueray No. Ten.

SEE ALSO

Citrus *p58*

Flavour profiles *p87*

Floral *p87*

Herbal *p128*

Juniper (common) *p137*

Juniper (other species) *p138*

London gin *p151*

Spicy *p212*

Tanqueray *p219*

Classic/Juniper-forward

| FLAVOUR PROFILE

Of course, all gins need to contain juniper and for London dry gin and distilled gins this should be the major flavour. However, some gins focus more heavily on the flavour of juniper and corresponding notes of pine and cedar. These gins are typically good all-rounders for mixing. Examples of such gins include Tanqueray, Hayman's London Dry, Palmers 44 and Crossbill.

SEE ALSO

Base spirit *p21*

Botanicals *p39*

Classic/Juniper-forward *p58*

Contemporary gin *p65*

Gordon's *p120*

London gin *p151*

Tanqueray *p219*

Transatlantic gin *p228*

Classic gin | GIN STYLE

A style of gin that is traditional and juniper-forward in flavour, reflecting the style of the dry gins made by British distillers in the mid-to late 19th century and 20th century. Gins such as Tanqueray, Gordon's and Beefeater are typical examples. The style was identified during the early 21st century, as the rise of newer, contemporary styles of gin led to a need

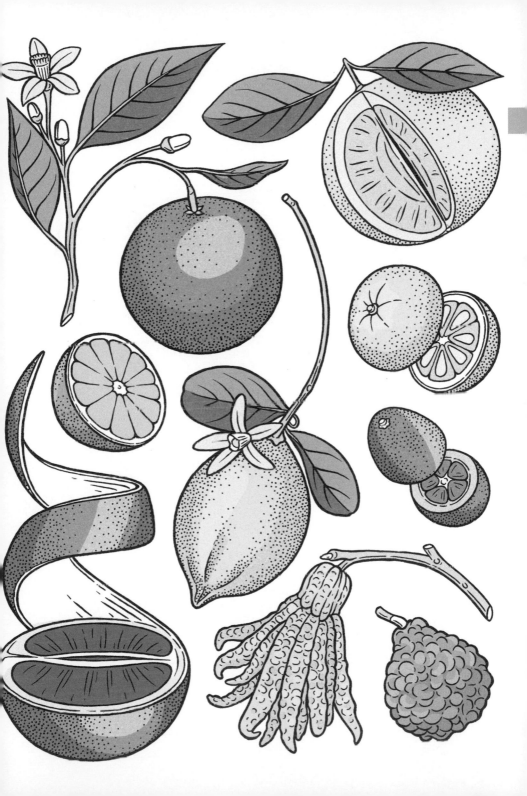

to differentiate the old style from the new ones. Another key component of classic gin is that it is made with a neutral base spirit, which adds little character to the gin and gives a blank canvas to the botanicals.

SEE ALSO
Dry vermouth *p80*
Glassware *p119*
Ice *p135*
Prohibition *p183*
Red vermouth *p191*
Shaken/Shaking *p201*

Clover Club | COCKTAIL

This pre-Prohibition cocktail was created in Philadelphia, USA, at the Bellevue-Stratford Hotel, a building that still exists and now houses Hyatt at The Bellevue. During the late 19th century, the hotel hosted the Clover Club, a gentleman's club of writers and lawyers whose membership included poet William Butler Yates. The cocktail likely dates from the early 20th century. The first recorded recipe was in Tom Bullock's *The Ideal Bartender* from 1917. However, by the repeal of Prohibition in 1933, the drink had lost a lot of its popularity and, because of its pale pink colour, was considered a particularly feminine drink. The Clover Club's fortunes were revived at the beginning of the 21st century, thanks to cocktail historian David Wondrich who wrote about it in 2007, and bartender Julie Reiner who opened a bar in Brooklyn named after the drink in 2009 and put the cocktail front-and-centre on her menu.

CLOVER CLUB RECIPE

50 ML / 2 FL OZ / LONDON DRY GIN
10 ML / ⅓ FL OZ / DRY VERMOUTH
5 ML / ⅕ FL OZ / RED VERMOUTH
5 ML / ⅕ FL OZ / RASPBERRY SYRUP
10 ML / ⅓ FL OZ / FRESH LEMON JUICE
1 EGG WHITE
1 RASPBERRY, TO GARNISH

Place all the ingredients in a cocktail shaker and shake well. Top up the shaker with ice cubes and shake again. Strain into a cocktail glass and garnish with a raspberry.

SEE ALSO
Botanical recipe *p36*
Botanicals *p39*
Cinnamon *p57*
Nutmeg *p168*
Spicy *p212*

Cloves SYZYGIUM AROMATICUM | BOTANICAL

Cloves are the immature, sun-dried flower buds of the clove tree, which can be used to flavour gins. The tree is evergreen and grows to up to 9m (30ft) in height, with narrow, white, bell-shaped flowers that turn pink when mature. Cloves are native to the spice islands of Indonesia, but are now also grown in Brazil, India, Jamaica, Malaysia and Tanzania. Cloves have a sweet, woody and spicy flavour due to their high concentration of eugenol. Eugenol has various medicinal and anaesthetic properties, and oil of clove has long been used to treat toothache. In cooking, cloves are used in a variety of sweet and savoury dishes and are often paired with other spices such as cinnamon and nutmeg. They also work well in concert with other spices in gin distilling, where they can be used to create a complex spice profile. As with cooking, cloves should be used sparingly, as they can easily overpower the botanical balance of the spirit. Cloves are also used in an assortment of liqueurs and as a key ingredient in spiced rum. Pink cloves are used to make the pink clove alcoholic cordial that is often mixed with rum or brandy. Gins that use cloves as a botanical include Bathtub Gin and Pickering's Gin.

SEE ALSO
ABV *p13*
Juniper (common) *p137*
Royal gin (Geneva) *p195*

Common gin | HISTORY

A term used to describe the adulterated gin served en-masse in ale houses during the late 18th and early 19th centuries. The following recipe for common gin is described in an 1805 handbook of distillation:

10 GALLONS MALT SPIRITS

2 OZ OIL OF TURPENTINE
1 LB JUNIPER BERRIES
4 OZ SWEET FENNEL
4 OZ CARAWAY SEED
3 HANDFULS BAY SALT

This spirit would have been proofed to the equivalent of 38% ABV. While the gin is made with juniper berries, the majority of the resinous, piney flavours characteristic of the berries would have come from the oil of turpentine, which is made from the distillation of pine resin.

Compounded gin | PRODUCTION

SEE ALSO
Base spirit *p21*
Botanicals *p39*
Ginebra San Miguel *p114*

Often simply referred to as "gin", compounded or cold compounded is a type of gin that is produced without any distillation of botanicals; instead, flavours are added directly to alcoholic spirit. The simplest and most inexpensive way to cold compound a gin is to purchase pre-made essential oils and mix these into neutral base spirit. The other way to make a cold compounded gin is to infuse a neutral base spirit with fresh or dried botanicals by immersing them in the spirit. The alcohol extracts the flavour and aroma compounds, as well as some colour from the botanicals. The advantages of compounding gin are the cheap initial capital outlay and low cost of production. The downside is that the resulting gin will be less consistent and less stable; it will change over time as the sediment from the botanicals drops out of solution. The flavour will also be different to a distilled product, as only certain botanical flavours and aromas are collected as part of a distillate. Examples of compounded gin include Cork Dry Gin and Ginebra San Miguel.

SEE ALSO

Aviation *p36*

Botanical recipe *p36*

Botanicals *p39*

Classic gin *p61*

Flavour profiles *p87*

Hendrick's *p127*

Juniper-forward *p139*

Martin Miller's *p156*

Transatlantic gin *p228*

Contemporary gin | GIN STYLE

A modern style of gin that has a less intense focus on the traditional, piney, juniper-forward flavour profile and a greater emphasis on the flavours of other botanicals such as citrus or spices. While these alternative botanicals may be more prominent than in many classic gins, it remains vital that juniper is still discernable for the spirit to be considered gin. The seeds for contemporary gin were sewn in the last few years of the 20th century. Distillers and gin brands were innovating and experimenting with flavour profiles, leading to the releases of gins such as Hendrick's, Martin Miller's, Tanqueray Malacca and Beefeater Wet. One of the first gins to identify itself as contemporary was Aviation, created by Ryan Magarian. Around 2009, Magarian coined the term "New Western Gin" to represent gins – such as Aviation – that had less of a focus on juniper. Another early contemporary gin, Bluecoat Gin, was released in 2006, described as "New American Dry". Contemporary gin is an umbrella term that covers both of these descriptions, along with others such as "New Wave Gin", "21st Century Gin" and "Modern Gin".

Contemporary gins have gained popularity with the renaissance in craft distilling, which has seen many new, small distilleries open across the world. These small enterprises cannot compete with more established brands on price; one way to differentiate themselves, among other factors, is with their flavour profile. Contemporary gins have also added to the recent success of gin by introducing new drinkers to the spirit, acting as a gateway and enabling them to explore and enjoy the category and a broader range of flavour profiles.

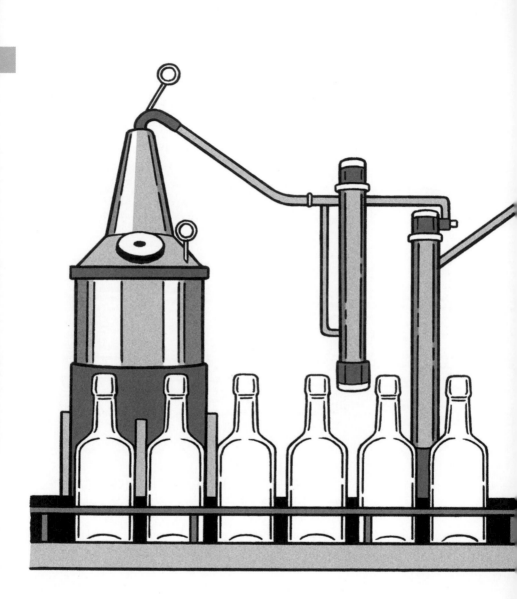

SEE ALSO
Botanicals p39
Distiller p76
Distillery p79

Contract distillers | PRODUCTION

Also known as third-party distillers, these are distillers that make gin for brands other than their own. This allows companies that do not wish to, or cannot afford to, start a distillery to still release a gin under their own label. The services offered by contract distillers vary, but include: allowing a competent distiller to rent time on their equipment; selling the company an "off the shelf" gin recipe; working with a company to develop a bespoke gin that is unique to them and has been tailored to their needs, for example, including a particular signature botanical that is not often found in gin. Distillers offering services to third parties include Thames Distillers Ltd (Timbermill Distillery), Alcohols Ltd (Langley Distillery), Artisan Spirits, English Spirit Distillery and G&J Distillers (Greenall's Distillery).

SEE ALSO
ABV p13
Botanical recipe p36
Fruit gin p92
Old Tom gin p171

Cordial gin | GIN STYLE

A type of gin which is sweetened, but is distinct from Old Tom gin. Old Tom gin was sweetened due to the impurities of the base spirit used to make it, but with the invention of continuous distillation in 1822, the quality and purity of base spirits increased significantly and sweetening was no longer necessary. Nevertheless, some consumers still wanted to indulge their sweet tooth. With gin now being able to be sold by the bottle and competition between distilleries increasing, some gin houses obliged. Cordial gins produced during the mid- to late 19th century were often designed with a botanical recipe that would work in harmony with the additional sugar content. Cordial gin was seen as the premier gin of the time and was typically available in two strengths: one for drinking neat and one with a higher alcoholic strength for mixing. As tastes moved towards dryer flavours and unsweetened gins, cordial gins disappeared. In 2016, Hayman Distillers released a new cordial gin at 42% ABV, which was designed to sit between the two historical strengths of cordial gin. They were followed by Sipsmith, who released a similar product in 2017. In the USA, cordial gin is defined as a liqueur with a "predominant characteristic flavour of gin". Bottled at 30% ABV or higher, it must not contain more than 2.5% wine.

SEE ALSO
Botanical recipe *p36*
Botanicals *p39*
Cilantro *p54*
Fixatives *p84*

Coriander seed *CORIANDRUM SATIVUM* | BOTANICAL

The second most important and prolific botanical used in gin production. Indeed, many 18th-century recipes call for equal amounts of juniper and coriander. Coriander seeds are typically small and round, and range in colour from brown to yellow. They have a citrus, spicy and sometimes floral quality which adds both body and intensity to gin. While coriander seed is native to southern Europe and North Africa, the region from which the botanical is sourced makes a big difference to its contribution to the gin's flavour. For example, coriander from Morocco has a subtle, floral spiced flavour; seeds from Russia have a high oil content and a citrus flavour; Indian coriander is lighter, with citrus and spice; and Canadian coriander has a more floral character. In addition to flavouring gin, coriander seed is also thought to have some fixative properties, helping to marry together the different botanical flavours and aromas in the spirit. Coriander seed is the key flavouring ingredient in the liqueur Parfait Amour and is also used in aquavit and Bénédictine.

SEE ALSO

Botanicals *p39*
Gin palace *p111*
Old Tom gin *p171*
Rotovap *p194*
Young Tom *p244*

Cream gin | HISTORY

A type of gin which originates from Victorian England. The main source of knowledge on this drink is the 1836 collection of short pieces by Charles Dickens, *Sketches by Boz*, in which the author describes the sight and sounds of a gin shop or gin palace. Dickens describes various barrels from which gin can be served, each containing a different variety. The barrels are given names including: "The Cream of the Valley", "The Out and Out", "The No Mistake", "The Good for Mixing" and "The Real Knock-me-down", in addition to "Old Tom", "Young Tom" and "Samson". The cream in "cream gin" does not refer to a dairy product, but rather that it is "the cream of the crop", the very best. As such, it uses the term in a similar way to the sherry Harvey's Bristol Cream. Nicholson's made a "celebrated Cream Gin" in the 1830s. Some modern-day distillers have taken a more literal approach by producing a gin that features cream as an ingredient. This started life as an in-house product at the Victorian-themed cocktail bar, Worship Street Whistling Shop in London, but was subsequently commercially produced by Atom Supplies. It uses cream as a botanical and is distilled in a rotovap. Each bottle contains the equivalent of 100ml (3½fl oz) of cream.

Crème de Genière | GIN STYLE

A cask-aged, juniper-flavoured liqueur. The term "crème" does not refer to any dairy products, but is rather an indication of the sweetness of the product in a similar way to Crème de Menthe (mint liqueur) or Crème de Mûre (blackberry liqueur). To be legally considered a "crème" in the European Union

SEE ALSO

ABV *p13*
Botanicals *p39*
Cordial gin *p67*
Juniper (common) *p137*

(EU), a liqueur must contain at least 250g (9oz) of sugar per 1 litre (1¾ pints) and be bottled at at least 15% ABV. Crème de Genième was popular during the late 19th century. It was made by distilling a single distillate of juniper with no other botanicals, before maturation in wooden casks for a period of 4–6 weeks; this would help to mellow the spirit. It would then be sweetened before being ready to serve. There are no commercially available Crème de Genièves currently made today, although the cask-aged version of the Hayman's Cordial Gin, made exclusively for the German market, comes very close.

SEE ALSO
Aviation *p20*

Crème de Violette | COCKTAIL INGREDIENT

This purple-hued liqueur is flavoured with violets. The "crème" in its name does not have anything to do with dairy, but rather indicates a minimum level of sweetness. The origins of Crème de Violette are found in the Ottoman Empire, where distillation was used to create floral essences. These techniques were transported to France by winemakers, who used them to flavour neutral alcohol for export to Syria. The first-known commercial Crème de Violette was sold in Philadelphia, USA in 1783. By the 19th century, Crème de Violette became popular with the nobility of Europe. One such noble, Alix of Hesse, the wife of Czar Nicholas II of Russia, was said to never drink coffee unless it contained the liqueur.

After further blips in popularity and reduced consumption during the First and Second World Wars, colourful liqueurs continued to be popular into the 1950s. By the 1960s, however, the production and distillation of Crème de Violette had reduced and it became an obscure

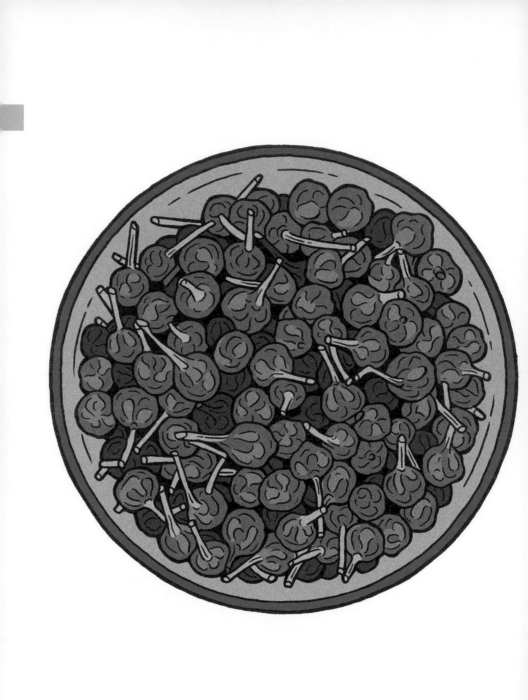

novelty that was only available in some corners of France. Shortly after, it disappeared completely. In 2006, Rothman & Winter began to export their Austrian version of the liqueur and, in 2009, The Bitter Truth of Germany released a Crème de Violette inspired by the original. Crème de Violette is a key ingredient in the following cocktails: Aviation, Eagle's Dream and Pousse Café.

Cubeb berries *PIPER CUBEBA* | BOTANICAL

SEE ALSO
Black peppercorn *p29*
Bombay Spirits Company *p33*
Botanical recipe *p36*
Botanicals *p39*
Grains of paradise *p123*

Also known as Java pepper, cubeb originates from Indonesia and is sometimes used as a botanical in gin production. The berries are typically dried for around four hours in a machine. After drying, they are visually very similar to black peppercorns, with the addition of a small tail. Cubeb has been used as a spice in Europe since the 4th century BC, where it was imported from Java. There are 9th-century records in the Middle East that refer to it as a seasoning and medicine. In distilling, cubeb berries are closely linked to grains of paradise and both botanicals feature in the recipes of Bombay Sapphire and Bombay Sapphire East. Cubeb berries add a fruity and floral pepper note, as well as a long and lingering menthol flavour, which is most notably evident on the finish.

Cucumber *CUCUMIS SATIVUS* | BOTANICAL

SEE ALSO
Botanicals *p39*
Fruit cups *p91*
Hendrick's *p127*
Martin Miller's *p156*
Pot distillation *p182*
Vacuum distillation *p233*
Vapour distillation *p234*

A member of the gourd family with long, thin, green fruits that have thin skin and sweet flesh. Cucumber is used extensively in drinks, from refreshing cucumber-infused water and cucumber-flavoured soft drinks to garnishes in fruit cups such as Pimm's. Cucumber has been an essential ingredient in both Hendrick's and

Martin Miller's Gin; in these, the cucumber is added after distillation as a concentrated essence. The distillation of cucumber is difficult as the flesh is sensitive to heat and, if overcooked, loses its fresh sweetness and becomes bitter and briney. For this reason, some distillers vacuum or vapour distil cucumber so that it is not exposed to as much heat as it is in pot distillation. Other distillers filter their gin through cucumber skin to add flavour. Farallon Gin of California, USA, filters the water that they will later use to proof their gin through cucumber.

Diamond method | MIXOLOGY

SEE ALSO
Ice *p135*
Martini *p159*
Shaken/Shaking *p201*
Stirred/Stirring *p215*

Made famous by Alessandro Palazzi of Dukes Hotel in London, this method of mixing drinks, especially Martinis, involves chilling the gin in the freezer beforehand, foregoing the need for any ice. Glasses are rinsed or spritzed with vermouth and the chilled gin is poured straight into the glass. Gin from the freezer is typically around −12°C (10°F), while gin at room temperature is around 20°C (68°F). The resulting drink is much colder and stronger, due to the lack of ice-melt diluting the gin. The texture of the gin is also thicker and more viscous – also a result of using colder gin. Critics of the drink suggest that it is little more than a glass of cold gin, but there is plenty of opportunity for theatrics. At Dukes Hotel, the drinks are made on a small trolley, served alongside the patrons' table. Because of the higher alcoholic strength and generous pours, guests at the hotel bar are strictly limited to two cocktails.

Dirty Martini | COCKTAIL

SEE ALSO
Martini *p159*
Shaken/Shaking *p201*

A variation on the Martini cocktail. While the classic Martini is often garnished with one or more olives, the Dirty Martini goes one step farther with the addition of olive brine to the shaker or glass before mixing. Additional olives are also added as a garnish. The drink has a briney, vegetal saltiness that helps to stimulate the appetite, making it a popular pre-dinner cocktail. An even more extreme variation, the Filthy Martini, features olives that are muddled into the shaker or mixing glass in addition to brine. It is essential to double-strain this cocktail to ensure a sediment-free drink. The origins of the Dirty Martini are thought to go back to 1901, when a Martini featuring muddled olives was served by John E O'Connor at the Waldorf Astoria hotel in New York City. During the Second World War, President Roosevelt was said to be a fan of a Martini made with a teaspoon of olive brine.

Distillation | PRODUCTION

See "Pot distillation", "Rectification", "Vapour distillation".

Distiller | PRODUCTION

SEE ALSO
Contract distillers *p67*
Distillery *p79*
Rectification *p187*

A person who participates in and oversees the production of gin (or other spirits) through distillation or rectification. Originally, in order to become a distiller, an individual would need to become an apprentice to a distiller already working in a distillery. Here, the apprentice would study under the supervision of a master, hence the term Master Distiller. With the consolidation of distilleries in the mid-20th century, the master and apprentice model fell out of use, although the title Master Distiller was still used to describe the most senior distiller in a distillery. Today, with a great increase in the number of distilleries, there has been a move to reserve the term for only the most experienced of distillers; essentially for those who are "masters of distilling". This either comes from

decades of experience or having the ability to distil or rectify a wide variety of different spirits. The terms Head Distiller or Distillery Manager are now often used for the most senior members of a distilling team. The Head Distiller is not necessarily involved in making the gin on a day-to-day basis; instead, they oversee the overall process. The everyday production is undertaken by the Production Distiller, who may be assisted by one or a number of Assistant Distillers.

SEE ALSO
Contract distillers *p67*
Distiller *p76*
Plymouth Gin *p178*

Distillery | PRODUCTION

The location where the equipment to distil and produce gin (or other spirits) is kept. For many gin brands, their distillery is owned and operated by the brand themselves, but some outsource the production of their gins to contract distillers. Distilleries will contain stills, blending tanks and often bottling operations; some of these are automated or semi-automated, whereas others are completely manual. In recent years, the concept of "destination distilling" has become more popular. This involves the distillery being open to the public, with the provision of distillery tours and the selling of spirits and souvenirs. As such, it becomes a "destination" for visitors. The ability to visit a distillery started with Plymouth Gin Distillery, but really took off in 2009 with the opening of Sipsmith Distillery in London. This shifted consumers' minds from simply how gins tasted to where they were made. Destination distilling not only offers additional revenue streams for gin brands, but also helps to build brand loyalty.

SEE ALSO
Martini *p159*
Red vermouth *p191*
Wormwood *p239*

Dry vermouth | COCKTAIL INGREDIENT

Also known as French vermouth, dry vermouth is an essential ingredient in many cocktails such as the Martini. It is a fortified wine flavoured with roots, herbs and spices, in particular, wormwood. The first recipe for dry vermouth, which would become Noilly Prat, was created by Joseph Noilly in Marseilles, France, in 1813. Joseph Chavasse created a dry vermouth recipe in 1821 that would become Dolin Dry Vermouth de Chambéry. Martini Extra Dry, from Italy, launched on New Year's Day in 1900.

Dry vermouth starts as a white wine, which is fortified with spirit, typically grape alcohol. After this, it is infused with a variety of botanicals. The exact blend of botanicals varies depending on the producer, but can include herbs, spices, flowers, roots and citrus peels. By law, it must also be flavoured with a species of the genus *Artemisia* (wormwood). While some sugar may be added to dry vermouth, it is significantly less than would be added to red or sweet vermouth. On its own, dry vermouth is typically drunk chilled or over ice as an aperitif, but it is perhaps most famous for being one of the two ingredients in a Dry Martini.

SEE ALSO
Botanical recipe *p36*
Botanicals *p39*
Hendrick's *p127*
Signature botanical gin *p202*

Elder *SAMBUCUS NIGRA* | BOTANICAL

A bushy tree (*Sambucus nigra*) with white flowers and black berries, common to most of Europe, sometimes referred to as the European or black elder. The berries have a jammy tartness and a light tanginess, while the frothy blossom has a lightly sweet and floral flavour, with a slight, straw-like quality. Both elderflower and elderberry are popular flavours in food and drink, especially in the UK and Nordic countries. Ripe elderberries are used to make a variety of jams, as well as being cooked in sauces. Both elderflowers and elderberries can also be fermented to make wine. Elderflower is a popular ingredient from which to make non-alcoholic cordial, as well as being the primary flavour of the liqueur St-Germain. In gin distilling, both elderflowers and elderberries are used, with the berries adding plump, jammy notes and the flowers bringing a light, lemony florality. Elderberries are relatively hardy, but care needs to be taken when distilling with the more delicate elderflower. Gins that feature elderflowers as a botanical include ShortCross Gin and Hendrick's Gin; those that use elderberries include ShortCross Gin and Conker Gin.

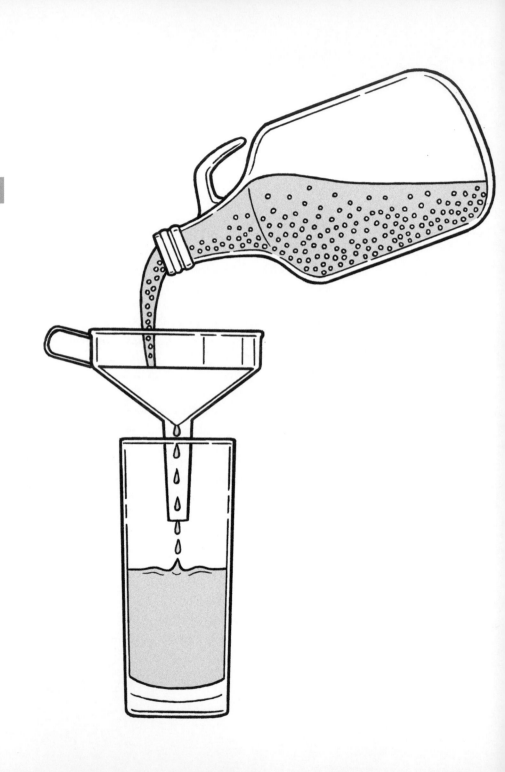

F

F

SEE ALSO
ABV *p13*

Filtration | PRODUCTION

After a gin has been distilled and proofed down to its bottling strength, it is important that it is filtered before bottling. It is also essential to ensure that the bottles that will receive the gin are clean and free of dust, which could cause undesirable particulates in the gin. Most gin distillers pass their gin through a 0.5 micron filter; this is a fine filter which will only allow the smallest particles through. One thousand microns are equivalent to 1mm, so a 0.5 micron filter will only allow through particles that are 0.0005mm in size or smaller.

Some distillers opt for the additional step, in terms of both cost and time, of chill filtration. This involves the spirit being cooled to between −10 and 4°C (14 and 39°F) and then passed through a fine filter. At this low temperature, any particulates in the spirit are likely to precipitate or fall out of solution and so are more easily caught by the filter. While chill filtering can reduce the possibility of hazing or cloudiness in the finished product, especially when ice, water or tonic are added, some critics argue that it also strips out some of the botanical complexity of a gin.

SEE ALSO
ABV *p13*
Distillery *p79*
London gin *p151*

Finsbury Gin | BRAND

Finsbury London Dry Gin was originally produced at the Finsbury Distillery in Finsbury, near Clerkenwell, a district of London just north of the City of London. The distillery was founded in 1740 by Joseph Bishop. The area was home to various distilleries, due in part to its access to the pure water of the Clerkenwell springs. Today, Finsbury Gin is owned by Borco International from Germany and is made in Still No. 7, also known as Jenny, a 10,000-litre (2,640-gallon) copper pot still at Langley Distillery, near Birmingham. Current expressions of Finsbury Gin include a version at 37.5% ABV, a rather intense bottling at 60% ABV, and the critically acclaimed Finsbury Platinum, bottled at 47% ABV.

SEE ALSO
Angelica root *p19*
Coriander seed *p68*
Nutmeg *p168*
Orris root *p174*

Fixatives | PRODUCTION

The flavour and aroma compounds within botanicals that give gin its character are, by their nature, volatile. If they had no volatility, then they would not distil easily. Volatility is the tendency for a substance to vaporize; for example, picture opening a bottle of gin – an exotic boutique of botanicals fills the air. This happens because those aromas are volatile and vaporize into the air, ready to be smelled and appreciated by the drinker. These escaping aromas make the bottle of gin inviting but, over time, mean that the complexity of the gin may fade. A similar problem exists in perfumery. The solution is to use fixatives, which help to bind flavours together and prevent a gin's volatiles (such as citrus) from evaporating.

A fixative is defined as being "used to equalize vapour pressure and thus the volatiles of the raw

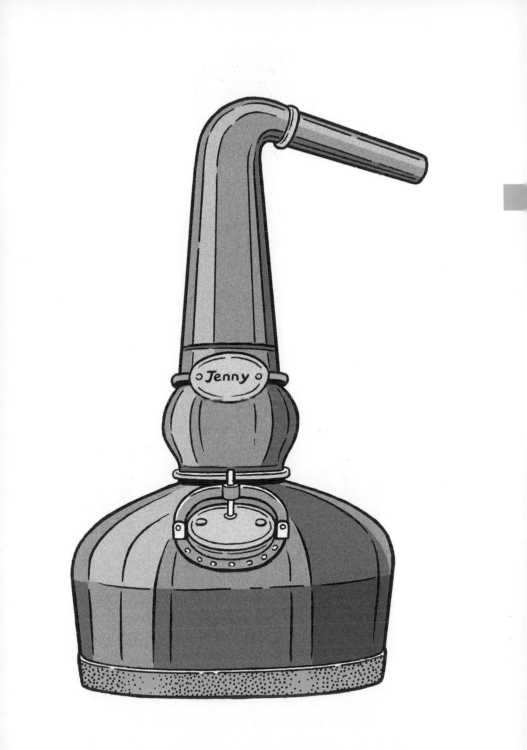

materials in a perfume oil as well as to increase its tenacity". Tenacity is the lasting effect of a character or flavour nuance. Fixatives have a high boiling point compared with the low ones of volatiles so, when they are mixed together, the fixatives make the liquid more disordered. Combined with the formation of some weak bonds known as Van der Waal bonds, this is what stops the volatiles from escaping so easily. When fixatives are used appropriately, a gin's flavour and aroma will be consistent over time. Examples of fixatives include coriander seed, angelica root, orris root and nutmeg.

Flavour profiles | PRODUCTION

....

The rough outline of a gin's flavour and aroma is known as its flavour profile. The vast range of botanicals used in gin production means that gins can taste very different from one another. In order to help communicate these differences to gin drinkers, authors, educators and gin companies have come up with a broad selection of flavour profile groups that most gins fit into. Examples include classic/juniper-forward, citrus, herbal, spicy and floral. It is worth noting that some gins may fit into more than one flavour profile group and that some individuals, because our sense of taste varies, may disagree with some categorizations.

SEE ALSO
Citrus p58
Classic/Juniper-forward p58
Floral p87
Herbal p128
Spicy p212

Floral | FLAVOUR PROFILE

....

Compared with the other standard flavour profiles of gin, this group covers a smaller number of products. Common floral botanicals include lavender (which works well with juniper and piney flavours), chamomile, rose and citrus blossom. The floral botanicals are often well

SEE ALSO
Botanical recipe p36
Cassia bark p50
Chamomile p53
Citrus p58
Flavour profiles p87
French 75 p88
Hendrick's p127
Juniper (common) p137
Lavender p143

Licorice root *p147*
Martini *p159*
Orris root *p174*
Rose *p192*

SEE ALSO
Glassware *p119*
Ice *p135*
Prohibition *p183*
Shaken/Shaking *p201*

complemented by additional botanical sweetness provided by licorice root, cassia root or orris root in the botanical recipe. Floral gins are often finely balanced, elegant and delicate. They work particularly well in short drinks such as the Gin Daisy, Martini and French 75. Examples of floral gins include Bloom, Geranium, Golden Moon, Silent Pool, Hendrick's and Nolet's Silver Dry Gin.

French 75 | COCKTAIL

An excellent choice for any celebration, this cocktail is a mix of Champagne, lemon juice and gin. The drink goes back to the 1920s, although similar drinks, such as the Champagne Cup, were recorded back in Victorian times. The first mention of the drink as the "French 75" was in the 1927 Prohibition-era book, *Here's How!* by Judge Jr, where it was described as being essentially a Tom Collins made with Champagne instead of soda water. The ingredients were to be added to a tall glass filled with ice and no shaking was required. The drink also features, with a nearly identical recipe, in the 1930 version of *The Savoy Cocktail Book* by Harry Craddock. The name of the cocktail is supposedly inspired by a French artillery field gun. This is often credited as the 75mm gun M1917, which was introduced in 1918. However, the Canon de 75 modèle 1897, which was produced until 1940, is a more likely candidate as this was a more prolific gun at the time and was known as both the "75" and the "French 75". Some modern recipes for the French 75 include the unnecessary step of shaking the first three ingredients, before serving the drink un-iced in a Champagne glass; it is worth noting that this can result in a warmer drink.

35ML / GENEROUS 1FL OZ / GIN
15ML / ½FL OZ / FRESH LEMON JUICE
15ML / ½FL OZ / SIMPLE SUGAR SYRUP
3–4 DASHES OF ORANGE BITTERS (OPTIONAL)
CHAMPAGNE, TO TOP UP

Fill a tall glass with ice, add the first three ingredients and stir. Drizzle with the bitters, if using, then top up with Champagne.

SEE ALSO
Ginger ale *p116*
Plymouth Gin *p178*
Red vermouth *p191*
Tonic water *p226*

Fruit cups | COCKTAIL INGREDIENT

A mix of spirit, fortified wine and other flavourings which is used as a form of pre-bottled punch to be diluted with a non-alcoholic mixer such as lemonade, ginger ale or tonic water. The diluted drink is often served from a well-iced jug or pitcher and garnished with various fruits, flowers and leaves such as lemon, lime, mint and borage. The most prolific fruit cup is Pimm's No.1, first released in 1840, which is made with a gin base and has inspired many other distilleries to release their own versions such as Plymouth Distillery, Sipsmith Distillery, New Columbia Distillers and Cotswolds Distillery. Fruit cups are made by a combination of maceration and distillation of botanicals with spirit. Wine, red vermouth, orange liqueur and ginger wine are common ingredients, too.

While most modern-day fruit cups are gin-based, variations based on other spirits have been released in the past. Pimm's released a range of expressions based on different spirits: Pimm's No.2 Cup (Scotch whisky base), released in 1851; Pimm's No.3 Cup (brandy base), released in 1851; Pimm's No.4 Cup (rum base), released in 1933; Pimm's No.5 Cup (Canadian rye whiskey base), released in Canada in the 1960s and the US and UK in 1964; and Pimm's No.6 Cup (vodka base), released in 1964. These variations were produced until 1970, when the company was sold to The Distiller's Company, which would later become part of Diageo. These additional cups were then discontinued, although No.6 was swiftly brought back (it was a favourite of the Chairman's wife) and remained in production until 2014.

Fruit gin | GIN STYLE

F

92

SEE ALSO
Gordon's *p120*
Sloe gin *p208*

A gin that has been flavoured by the infusion of fresh or dried fruit. Fruit gins are often sweetened, sometimes with the addition of fruit juice. The most famous fruit gin is probably sloe gin, which is technically a category in its own right and is classified as a liqueur. Fruit gins have been made on a domestic scale for centuries and were often used as a way to preserve excess fruit. In the UK, fruit gins were made from country and hedgerow fruit and berries such as sloes, damsons and blackberries. Commercial varieties of fruit gin became available by the early 20th century, with orange and lemon gins being some of the most popular flavours. Gordon's produced an orange and a lemon gin for nearly 60 years. In Scotland, apple gin, made by infusing the soluble parts of an apple in gin, was particularly popular. Other popular flavours of the period included passionfruit, pineapple, maple, celery and asparagus. By the 1960s, these products had become less popular and many were discontinued; the last lemon gin was produced until 1988. At the beginning of the 21st century, fruit gins began to make a comeback with the return of orange gin accompanied by new flavours such as elderflower, rhubarb, cherry and pineapple.

G

SEE ALSO
Botanical recipe *p36*
Botanicals *p39*
Citrus *p58*
Coriander seed *p68*
Ginger *p114*
Juniper (common) *p137*
Pinene *p177*

Galangal *ALPINIA GALANGA* | BOTANICAL

Also known as blue or Thai ginger, galangal is a rhizome, a subterranean stem, that is closely related to common ginger and part of the Zingiberaceae family. It is used as a botanical to flavour some gins. Galangal is native to Indonesia, but also grows in the Philippines, Laos, Malaysia and Thailand. The botanical looks similar to ginger root, but has a darker, pink-brown skin. At one time, galangal was a popular gin botanical, likely due to its flavour of citrus and pine, which naturally complements other gin botanicals such as juniper, coriander and citrus peels. It contains the oil galangol, which breaks down during distillation to produce chemical compounds including pinene, cineol and eugenol. Gin 1495 Verbatim and Gin 1495 Interpretation use galangal as a botanical.

SEE ALSO
Gin & Tonic *p104*
Gin Tonica *p113*

Garnishes | COCKTAIL INGREDIENT

The finishing touch that, when added to a cocktail, improves the look, aroma and taste of the drink. The most popular type of garnish is citrus fruit – usually lemon, lime, orange or grapefruit – prepared in one of a number of different ways. A wedge is cut vertically, end-to-end from the citrus fruit and either placed in the drink or on the side of the glass. A wheel is a horizontal slice cut across the entire diameter of the fruit, while a twist is a piece of the rind which is peeled away from the pith and squeezed over the drink so that the oils in the peel are expressed (sprayed over the drink).

There is some debate over whether to use lemon or lime for a Gin & Tonic. Lemon is sweeter and so tends to work well with more classic, dryer gins, while the tartness of lime is a good contrast to the sweet flavour profiles of some contemporary gins. A compromise – the use of both lemon and lime – is known as the Evans Gin & Tonic. Other garnishes often used in gin cocktails include olives, cocktail onions, cucumber slices, basil leaves, sprigs of rosemary and chocolate shavings.

SEE ALSO
ABV *p13*

Genever | GIN STYLE

Also known as jenever or Geneva gin, this spirit originates from the Netherlands. Genever is named after the Dutch for juniper, *jeneverbes*. Genever has a characterful base spirit made from malt wine (*moutwijn*); this is made from a variety of grains such as rye, malted barley or corn. The spirit is produced in a similar way to whiskey in that it is triple or quadruple distilled in pot stills. There are four main styles of genever.

Jonge genever is a modern style first developed in the 1950s to be light and easier to mix in cocktails. It is closer to gin and contains less malt wine than other styles. This style must, technically, be bottled at 35% ABV and contain no more than 15% malt wine and 10g (⅓oz) of sugar per litre (1¾ pints).

The name of Oude genever reflects the older style, rather than the age of the spirit itself. These genevers are more botanically intense, with more of the flavour of the base spirit coming

through. Oude genever must technically be bottled at least 35% ABV, contain no more than 20g (⅔oz) of sugar per litre (1¾ pints) and contain at least 15% malt wine. If an Oude genever is labelled as aged, it must have been aged for at least a year in a barrel of 700 litres (154 gallons) or smaller in size.

Korenwijn, also known as corn or grain wine, must technically contain at least 51% malt wine and be bottled at at least 38% ABV. The maximum amount of sugar allowed per litre (1¾ pints) is 20g (⅔oz).

The final category contains the fruit-flavoured genevers, which tend to be less botanically intense and have a more neutral base.

Gibson | COCKTAIL

SEE ALSO
Dry vermouth *p80*
Martini *p159*
Umami *p231*

A variation on the Martini cocktail; the main point of difference is the use of a cocktail onion or two as the garnish. There are numerous origin stories for this cocktail, although it seems likely that it was invented in the Bohemian Bar by businessman Walter D K Gibson. The onion adds a lot of flavour, with lots of savoury and umami notes. Cocktail onions are usually pearl onions (*Allium ampeloprasum* var. *sectivum*), also known as button or baby onions. They have a natural sweetness and are pickled with small quantities of spices such as pepper, paprika and turmeric. Some cocktail onions are also pickled in vermouth instead of brine or vinegar and can therefore be used to add a tiny splash of vermouth to the Martinis of drinkers who prefer a very dry Gibson.

SEE ALSO
ABV *p13*
Gin house *p107*

Gilbey's | BRAND

A true classic of Britain's gin heritage and a gin brand that continues to remain popular, especially in some Commonwealth markets, to this day. Gilbey's Gin was founded in 1872 by Walter and Alfred Gilbey. The brothers were introduced to the industry by another brother, Henry Gilbey, who was a partner in a wine merchants. The gin was produced at the Gilbey Distillery in Camden Town, London. Over time, Gilbey's diversified and purchased a selection of Scotch whisky distilleries as well as Croft's Port. Given the success of the gin brand prior to the Second World War, satellite distilleries were opened in Australia and Canada. Throughout its history, Gilbey's has been bottled at between 37.5% and 47.4% ABV. There was also a Gilbey's Antique Gin, which was based on an old recipe and bottled at 43% ABV. While the brand is now owned by Diageo, Gilbey's is produced and sold under a long-term licence by Beam Suntory.

Gimlet | COCKTAIL

A shaken gin drink made from equal parts gin and lime cordial; the latter is sometimes substituted for a mix of fresh lime juice and sugar syrup. Traditionally, Plymouth Gin and Rose's Cordial are used. The drink has strong naval connections and it is likely that it is named after a tool used to pierce holes in barrels, although some sources suggest that it is named after a former Surgeon Admiral, Sir Thomas Gimlette. Lime juice was given to sailors to help prevent scurvy, and lime cordial was a way to preserve fresh lime juice for long voyages. The earliest written reference to the Gimlet was in

SEE ALSO
Glassware *p119*
Ice *p135*
Plymouth Gin *p178*
Shaken/Shaking *p201*

May 1927 in the *Portsmouth Evening News*. The article describes a Lieutenant from the Royal Navy who was arrested, having been accused of driving when drunk. The officer had consumed "six or seven Gimlets". When asked what these were, the Lieutenant described them as a drink made from "gin, lime juice and water".

GIMLET RECIPE

50ML / 2FL OZ / DRY GIN (IDEALLY PLYMOUTH DRY GIN)
20ML / ⅔FL OZ / LIME CORDIAL

Place the ingredients into a cocktail shaker filled with ice, shake well and strain into a cocktail glass.

Gin Act 1729 | HISTORY

The Gin Acts were a series of laws put into place in the United Kingdom during the 18th century to help stem the abuse of gin and the social, criminal and health problems that it was causing. The initial attempt to reduce gin consumption in 1729 required retailers to purchase an annual licence and added an excise duty of 5 shillings per gallon on gin. One of the aims of the new costs was to encourage the export of domestic spirit. Wealthy landowners, whose grain was often used by distillers to make the base spirit of gins, were concerned about the potential loss of income. One issue with the act was that it specifically focused on gin, which was defined as being made using "juniper berries, or other fruit, spices or ingredients" so the law could easily be circumvented by leaving out the botanicals. This raw alcohol became known as "Parliamentary Brandy".

SEE ALSO
Base spirit *p21*
Common gin *p64*
Gin Act 1736 *p101*
Gin Act 1751 *p101*
Gin house *p107*
Gin Lane *p108*

SEE ALSO
Common gin *p64*
Gin Act 1729 *p100*
Gin Act 1751 *p101*
Gin Lane *p108*

Gin Act 1736 | HISTORY

After the failure of the Gin Act of 1729, a new act was designed to curb the consumption of gin. As before, this new act (also known as the Spirits Duties Act of 1735) included an annual licence fee for retailers and an excise tax on gin. The excise tax was 20 shillings per gallon (approximately £27 per litre (1¾ pints) in 2017 prices) and the licence fee was £50 (about £6,070 in 2017 prices). The licence drove gin production underground and few licences were issued. Enforcement of the act was weak and gin production increased.

By the 1740s, Britain was involved in a full-scale war on the continent caused by a dispute over Maria Theresa's succession to the throne within the Habsburg Monarchy. The dispute involved almost all of the major powers within Europe. The fighting was not confined to the European continent, but spread to India and the British colonies in North America, too. The immense financial pressure of this global war led to the repeal of this gin act in 1743 (with the new Gin Act of 1743). The excise duty on gin was reduced and the retail licence was reduced to £1, a reduction of 98 percent.

SEE ALSO
Gin Act 1729 *p100*
Gin Act 1736 *p101*
Gin house *p107*
Gin Lane *p108*

Gin Act 1751 | HISTORY

This parliamentary act (also known as the Sales of Spirits Act 1750) was passed in the United Kingdom in response to rising incidents of robberies and murders, which were linked by a parliamentary committee to the increase in gin consumption. Petitions from many London parishes, as well as the major towns of Bristol, Manchester and Norwich, called on the government to pass regulation. Unlike previous laws, this act focused on gin producers,

rather than retailers. The act made it illegal for gin distillers to sell their spirits to unlicensed merchants. The licence for retailers was set at £2 and could only be issued to individuals who were payers of rent and rates. These two measures put many small gin shops and sellers out of business and consolidated the gin business to the larger and more established merchants. The act was successful. In 1751, consumption of gin in the UK was 38.6 million litres (8.5 million gallons); this fell to 26.8 million litres (5.9 million gallons) in 1752 and again to 9.5 million litres (2.1 million gallons) by 1760.

SEE ALSO

Bush gin *p43*
Citrus *p58*
Classic/Juniper-forward *p58*
Contemporary gin *p65*
Flavour profiles *p87*
Fruit gin *p92*
Garnishes *p93*
Gin Tonica *p113*
Glassware *p119*
Gordon's *p120*
Ice *p135*
Uganda Waragi *p231*

Gin & Cola | COCKTAIL

A drink made by combining gin and cola in a similar way to a Gin & Tonic. While the mixed drink's popularity is currently limited to the USA and Europe, it is gradually increasing. The practice of drinking gin with cola is particularly common with the brand Uganda Waragi from Africa; Coca Cola is something of a luxury item and so drinking gin with it is a status symbol. In the rest of the world, the emergence of contemporary styles of gins with bold flavour profiles which are less juniper-forward has led to experimentation with different flavours and drinks. These new gins are well complemented by the herbal and spice aromatics of cola, in particular bush gins and those with a greater citrus character. Fruit gins, such as those flavoured with strawberry, pineapple and cherry, are also commonly mixed with cola. The result is an accessible drink that appeals to new gin drinkers and is a good starting point from which to start exploring gin. Despite the contemporary feel of the Gin & Cola, there are references to the combination dating back to at least 1927, when

Judge Jr's *Here's How!* details the "Southern Exposure": a 50/50 mix of Gordon's Gin and Coca Cola served over cracked ice.

GIN & COLA RECIPE

50ML / 2FL OZ / GIN
150ML / 5FL OZ / COLA
1 DASH OF ORANGE BITTERS
CITRUS FRUITS, TO GARNISH

Fill a tall glass (or Gin Tonica glass) with ice, add all the ingredients and garnish with a medley of citrus fruits.

Gin & Tonic | COCKTAIL

SEE ALSO
Gin Tonica *p113*
Glassware *p119*
Ice *p135*
Quininated gin *p185*
Quinine *p185*
Tonic water *p226*

The first written reference to the Gin & Tonic was in an 1868 edition of *The Oriental Sporting Magazine* in which the writer recounts a story of horse racing in Sialkot, which is today part of the Punjab province in Pakistan, but was then part of British India. The original Gin & Tonic would have been drunk, in part, for medical reasons commonly accepted at the time. The quinine of the tonic water warded off malaria, while the gin was thought to aid digestion. Any citrus added would have helped to prevent scurvy. Early Gin & Tonics would have likely been a murky mixture of powdered cinchona bark, sugar for sweetening, lime juice and gin, with still or sparkling water added afterwards. After the quinine sulphate (quinine in crystal form) was isolated from the bark, it would have been possible to instead ship a box of these "quinine grains" to various colonial outposts of the British Empire and for drinkers to add a single grain to a bottle of soda water to make their tonic. By the late 19th century, officers and administrators returning from the Empire brought the taste back home with them to the UK, although it remained an obscure drink

in the United States, even into the 1930s. This changed when Schweppes issued a franchise to the Metropolitan Bottling Company in the 1950s, accompanied by an advertising campaign. At this time, tonic water was still called quinine water in the United States. The Gin & Tonic continued to be a popular drink throughout the second half of the 20th century. Recent innovations in serves, tonic waters and gin itself have rejuvenated the drink, a specific example being the Spanish-style Gin Tonica serve, which allows for great creativity and customization.

GIN & TONIC RECIPE

50ML / 2FL OZ / DRY GIN
150ML / 5FL OZ / CHILLED TONIC WATER
LEMON AND LIME SLICES, TO GARNIGH

Fill a chilled tumbler or highball glass with ice. Add the gin, then top up with tonic water. Garnish with lemon and lime.

Gin Guild | HISTORY

SEE ALSO
Worshipful Company of
Distillers *p239*

Founded in 2013 with close connections to the Worshipful Company of Distillers, the Gin Guild aims to "celebrate excellence in gin distillation and promotion". Membership is made up of a collection of distillers, brand owners, bartenders, writers and journalists from around the world. The Gin Guild is also a repository of gin-related information and runs an annual one-day conference, the Ginposium, as well as a selection of other talks and tastings throughout the year.

Gin house | HISTORY

SEE ALSO
Booth's *p34*
Burrough's *p42*
Gilbey's *p98*
Gin Act 1729 *p100*
Gin palace *p111*

The term "gin house" refers to a number of gin brands and distilleries that were established in the 18th and 19th centuries. They led gin's

Gordon's *p120*
Greenall's *p126*
Tanqueray *p219*

SEE ALSO
Common gin *p64*
Gin Act 1729 *p100*
Gin Act 1736 *p101*
Gin Act 1751 *p101*

return to respectability after the Gin Craze. Most gin houses were based in London, family owned and named after the individual who founded them. Many of gin's biggest names are historical gin houses and many continue to exist in one form or another. Examples include Booth's (founded in London around 1740 by John Booth), Burnett's (founded in 1770 in London by Sir Robert Burnett), Burrough's (founded in 1862 in Chelsea, London, by James Burrough), Gilbey's (founded in 1872 in Camden Town, London, by Walter and Alfred Gilbey), Gordon's (founded in 1769 in London by Alexander Gordon), Greenall's (founded in 1761 by Thomas Dakin), Warrington (purchased by G&J Greenall – now G&J Distillers – in 1870) and Tanqueray (founded in 1830 in Bloomsbury, London, by Charles Tanqueray).

Gin Lane | HISTORY

One of a set of two contrasting prints, the other being *Beer Street*, which were created by artist William Hogarth (1697–1764) in 1751. *Gin Lane* portrays the "evil" of gin, while *Beer Street* illustrates the supposed "benefits" of drinking beer. The two prints were engraved by Hogarth who then sold copies of them on for a guinea for the set. In the initial subscription, 1,240 were sold. *Gin Lane*, set in the parishes of either St Giles or St James in London, shows a range of thievery, skullduggery and drunkenness. Both the people and the buildings are in a state of disrepair and decay, and only the pawnbrokers is thriving. In contrast, *Beer Street* shows the buildings in a fine state of repair, except for the tumbledown pawnbrokers. The people are portrayed as happy, civilized and contented.

The prints were a visual aid to support the argument that many of the time were making against the evils of gin. The Gin Craze was well established in Great Britain during this period, especially in London. There was a sharp increase in the production and consumption of gin, but limited regulation and poor-quality product led to an epidemic of drunkenness and increases in crime and disorder. During the first half of the 18th century, many in the middle and upper classes were campaigning for the government to respond, which they eventually did in the form of a series of Acts of Parliament known as the Gin Acts.

SEE ALSO
ABV *p13*
Crème de Genièvre *p71*
Fruit gin *p92*
Sloe gin *p208*

Gin liqueurs | GIN STYLE

Products that use gin as their base, but have been flavoured and sweetened after distillation. In order to be considered a liqueur (within the European Union, at least), a product must contain 100g (3½oz) of sugar per litre (1¾ pints). Most typical gin liqueurs are similar to fruit gin, where a gin has been infused with fruit or other ingredients, before being sweetened; the product takes on the aromas, flavours and often the colour of the ingredients. Popular flavours include rhubarb, orange, sloe, damson and elderflower. Gin liqueurs often have lower alcoholic strength than gins. In the EU, they must be a minimum of 15% ABV, compared with a minimum of 37.5% ABV for gin. Most commercially available gin liqueurs sit between 20% and 30% ABV, although over the last few years there has been a recent rise in popularity of "full strength" gin liqueurs bottled at 40% ABV. Many fruit gins could also be considered gin liqueurs.

SEE ALSO
Common gin *p64*
Gin house *p107*
Gin Lane *p108*

Gin palace | HISTORY

The gin shops of the mid-18th-century Gin Craze
were small, seedy, unlicensed establishments.
Unscrupulous landlords would often water
down and then adulterate gin with substances
as unpleasant as oil of vitriol (sulphuric acid)
so that the gin still had a kick. In contrast
to these dark, dingy dens, the gin palaces of
the mid-18th century were places of gaiety
and light. Gin palaces were created in part in
response to brewers who were investing heavily
in public houses to make them more attractive
to the passing trade and the rising middle
classes, buoyed by the success of the Industrial
Revolution. Another result of the Industrial
Revolution, gas lighting, allowed the gin palaces
to become bright establishments, often aided by
plenty of gilding and sparkling mirrors. One of
the best accounts of a gin palace is from *Sketches
by Boz* written by Charles Dickens in the 1830s.
In this, Dickens describes plate glass windows,
gilt gas burners and ornamental mirrors; a place
that was "perfectly dazzling" in stark contrast
to "the darkness and dirt" of the outside world.
Gin palaces offered drinkers comfortable
surroundings that were light, bright and – most
importantly during the winter months – warm;
something that they might not have had at home.

SEE ALSO
Gimlet *p98*
Glassware *p119*
Ice *p135*
Soda water *p208*

Gin Rickey | COCKTAIL

Also known as a Lime Rickey, this simple cocktail
started life as a Bourbon whiskey cocktail, rather
than a gin one. It was invented in the 1880s as
a long, thirst-quenching cocktail and named
after the lobbyist, broker and Civil War veteran,
Colonel Joe Rickey, who hailed from Fulton,
Missouri. The drink was created in Shoomaker's

Bar on Pennsylvania Avenue in Washington DC. The bar was frequented by various politicians, lawmakers and journalists, which was why it was a key hang-out for lobbyists. By the 1890s, a variation on the original cocktail had emerged, which replaced the Bourbon with gin. This adds a botanical complexity and makes the drink slightly drier. Most gins will work well in a Gin Rickey, but for added authenticity, choose one of the great gins produced by a distillery in Washington DC, such as Green Hat Distillery, Joseph A Magnus & Co., One Eight Distilling, or District Distilling Co. If the drink is too tart, you can always add some sugar to sweeten it.

GIN RICKEY RECIPE

50ML / 2FL OZ / DRY GIN
15ML / ½FL OZ / FRESH LIME JUICE
CLUB SODA OR SPARKLING WATER, TO TOP UP

Fill a tall glass with ice, add the gin and lime juice, and stir. Top up with soda or sparkling water.

Gin Tonica | COCKTAIL

....

The Spanish-style serve of the Gin & Tonic, which is now considered a drink in its own right as a result of its popularity. The drink requires a large, stemmed "goldfish bowl" glass, although a large burgundy glass is sometimes used. The glass is filled with plenty of ice before a generous measure of gin is added, followed by tonic. The Gin Tonica utilizes a great range of colourful, aromatic and imaginative garnishes, which are often matched to the specific pairing of gin and tonic. The large amount of ice in the drink helps to keep it cold throughout the hot Spanish summers and the stemmed glassware prevents the drinker's hands from heating up the drink. The Gin Tonica originated in 2008 in the Basque

SEE ALSO
Garnishes p93
Gin & Tonic p104
Glassware p119
Ice p135
Tonic water p226

region of Europe and was popular with local Michelin star chefs who needed to keep cool during kitchen service. The popularity of the Gin Tonica has led to a range of accessories being added to the market, such as pots of botanicals for garnishes, botanical infusion tea bags and a wide range of flavoured tonic waters.

Ginebra San Miguel | BRAND

The world's best-selling gin, which is produced in the Philippines and almost exclusively consumed there; very little of the product is available for export. The company is owned by the San Miguel Corporation, which is based in Manila. Ginebra San Miguel currently make three gin-related products: their original red label, bottled at 40% ABV and flavoured with juniper and other essences; a "Premium" offering bottled at 35% ABV, which features juniper, lemon and lime, among other botanicals; and GSM Blue, which is described as a "cane alcohol blended with essence of juniper and other botanicals" and is bottled at 32.5% ABV. Technically, only the red label can be considered gin in the European Union and United States. All products in the current range are produced by cold compounding spirit with botanical essences and flavourings; no botanicals are distilled. Both the red label and premium varieties taste like very light examples of gin and are often embellished by the consumer; popular examples include the placing of chilli peppers or other spices or herbs into the bottle to infuse.

Ginger *ZINGIBER OFFICINALE* | BOTANICAL

A member of the Zingiberaceae (ginger family) along with cardamom and galangal, ginger is also commonly used as a botanical

SEE ALSO
ABV *p13*
Botanicals *p39*
Compounded gin *p64*
Juniper (common) *p137*
Lemon *p143*
Lime (Persian) *p148*

SEE ALSO
Botanical recipe *p36*
Botanicals *p39*
Cardamom *p49*
Galangal *p93*
Ginger ale *p116*

Ginger wine *p117*
Gordon's *p120*

SEE ALSO
Ginger *p114*
Gordon's *p120*

in gin production. The exact origin of ginger is unknown, although many botanists believe that it originated in India. Ginger is a flowering plant, although it is the root that is of interest to cooks and distillers. The part of the plant referred to as the root is actually a rhizome (subterranean stem), which is available in fresh, dried, powdered or pickled forms. Ginger has a spicy heat due to the presence of the chemical compound gingerol, which is related to capsaicin and piperine, the chemicals that give black pepper and chilli pepper their heat. Capsaicin is sometimes added to ginger-flavoured dishes and products (especially ginger beer) to increase their heat as it is cheaper than ginger. In drinks, ginger is the key flavour of ginger wine, ginger ale and ginger beer. In gin production, it can be used as a botanical to add spice notes and a sweet, cosy warmth, although the flavour and heat of ginger is much more subtle when distilled than when in its raw or powdered forms. Examples of gins that use ginger include Campfire Gin, Gordon's Distiller's Cut and Opihr Gin.

Ginger ale | COCKTAIL INGREDIENT

A carbonated, sweetened soft drink flavoured with ginger. Unlike ginger beer, it is not produced by the fermentation of ginger with yeast and sugar, but is simply flavoured with the spice. Ginger ale is generally golden in colour and clear, whereas ginger beer is often cloudy because of the fermentation process. In addition to ginger, other flavourings are sometimes used, including other spices and fruit, such as lemon or lime. There are two types of ginger ale: Belfast style, a heavier, sweeter style with a strong ginger flavour that dates back to 19th-century Northern Ireland; and dry ginger ale, which is a lighter style attributed to John J McLaughlin, chemist, pharmacist and the founder of Canada Dry. McLaughlin founded a soda water bottling plant in Toronto in 1890 and, around 1904, had declared his desire to make "the Champagne of ginger ale"; he patented Canada Dry Ginger Ale in 1907. The dry style gained in popularity throughout the 20th century, in particular because of its mixability with spirits and the rise of the cocktail hour. Other popular brands include Schweppes, Seagram's and Fever-Tree. Popular mixed drinks involving gin and ginger ale include the Gin Buck (gin and ginger ale, often garnished with lemon) and The Padlock (equal parts Gordon's Gin and ginger ale, referenced in Judge Jr's *Here's How* in 1927). The introduction to The Padlock states, "This drink is very popular because it's so easy to mix if you are out dancing. In fact, you can mix it in the ginger ale bottles at home and put them right up on the table".

Ginger wine | COCKTAIL INGREDIENT

Ginger wine is a fortified wine made from fermented ginger root and raisins. The earliest reference to the drink tells of its production at the Finsbury Distilling Company in 1740. One of the distillery's major customers was grocer Joseph Stone, who was based in High Holborn, London. Stone's Ginger Wine is still made today and is bottled at 13.5% ABV. A sweeter and stronger "Special Reserve" is bottled at 18% ABV. Ginger wine is sometimes drunk neat over ice, but is also a common ingredient in fruit cups and other cocktails such as the Cushing Cocktail (2 parts gin and 1 part ginger wine, shaken with ice).

SEE ALSO
ABV *p13*
Finsbury Gin *p84*
Fruit cups *p91*
Ginger *p114*

SEE ALSO
ABV *p13*
Base spirit *p21*
Botanical recipe *p36*
Botanicals *p39*
Charge *p54*
Contemporary gin *p65*
Genever *p94*
Hybrid gin *p132*
London gin *p151*
Pot distillation *p182*

Ginniver | GIN STYLE

Similar in many ways to a hybrid gin, Ginniver sits firmly between a Genever and a dry gin. It has the malty character of a Dutch Genever, but the botanical complexity and dryness of a modern gin. Ginnivers are typically made by distilleries that also produce whiskey and are most common in the United States of America, with the distillery using their unaged whiskey (or "white dog", as it is known) as the gin's base spirit. The botanical recipes tend to be relatively simple, containing only five or six botanicals, as the base spirit itself adds a lot of character and almost acts like a botanical in its own right. As the white dog used for the base spirit of the gin is likely to have been pot distilled, it is unlikely that it will have been distilled up to 96% ABV, thus making it ineligible to be sold in the European Union (EU) as gin. As a solution, some distillers will add a small proportion of Neutral Grain Spirit (NGS) that has been distilled to 96% ABV to the still's charge, thus satisfying the EU regulation. Examples of Ginnivers or Ginniver-like gins include FEW American Gin and Copperworks.

SEE ALSO
Aviation *p20*
Gin & Tonic *p104*
Gin Tonica *p113*
Ice *p135*
Martini *p159*
Negroni *p168*

Glassware | MIXOLOGY

The collective term for the various types of glass used to drink and enjoy gin. These include the Tasting Glass, a small, typically tulip-shaped glass with a small bowl which narrows at the lip. This helps to concentrate the aromas of botanicals. Tasting glasses are available in both stemmed and unstemmed versions. Popular examples include those produced by Glencairn and Bugatti. The Martini Glass, sometimes referred to more generally as a cocktail glass, is a stemmed glass with a V-shaped bowl. The stem helps to keep the heat from the drinker's hand from warming the drink. These are often used for Martinis, Aviations, Sweet Martinis and White Ladies.

The Tumbler is a short glass that fits comfortably in the hand and often has a heavy base. This glass is used for short drinks such as the Negroni and the Bramble. It is also a popular choice for some for the Gin & Tonic. The Hiball or Highball is a tall glass to be used for long drinks that need to be served with plenty of ice, drinks such as the Collins, Singapore Sling, Long Island Iced Tea and, in some cases, the Gin & Tonic. The way that the ice stacks in the glass means that, initially, the cubes melt more slowly. The Gin Tonica is a tall, stemmed glass with a large bowl, typically big enough to hold 600ml (1 pint) of liquid. The glass needs to be big to contain the vast amount of ice called for by the Gin Tonica.

SEE ALSO

ABV *p13*
Angelica root *p19*
Botanical recipe *p36*
Botanicals *p39*
Coriander seed *p68*
Fruit gin *p92*
Gin house *p107*
Juniper (common) *p137*
Licorice root *p147*
London gin *p151*
Old Tom gin *p171*
Tanqueray *p219*
Vesper *p237*

Gordon's | BRAND

A major gin brand from England that has produced gin since the 18th century. They produce a classic London dry gin, which is sold at a variety of strengths. The UK version has a distinctive green glass bottle, but export varieties are sold in clear bottles. Its botanical recipe includes juniper, coriander seed, angelica root and licorice root. Gordon's also produce a sloe gin and a number of flavoured gins. Notable discontinued products include an Old Tom gin, orange gin, lemon gin and a range of pre-mixed cocktails in shaker-themed bottles. The company was founded in London in 1769 by Alexander Gordon, originally from Scotland. The company moved to Clerkenwell,

London, in 1786 and continued to be owned by
the Gordon family until 1847, when Charles
Gordon sold it to John Currie & Co., a producer
of neutral spirit whose customers included,
among others, Tanqueray. In 1898, Gordon's and
Tanqueray merged, forming the single biggest
gin producer in England. In 1922, the company
was acquired by The Distillers Company Ltd.
This was later taken over by Guinness & Co. to
become United Distillers, which is now a part
of Diageo. Gordon's opened their first distillery
in the United States in 1934. They also opened
distilleries in Canada, South America and
Jamaica. In 1998, their UK gin production
moved to Cameronbridge Distillery in Scotland.

Today, Gordon's London Dry Gin is produced
and distributed around the world. The strength
varies depending on the market: 37.5% ABV in
the United Kingdom, 40% ABV in the United
States and 47.3% ABV in continental Europe
and for UK Duty Free. Gordon's has made
notable appearances in popular culture for
many years, including in the novels by Ian
Fleming, where the Vesper cocktail is made with
Gordon's. They also have a well-documented
history of advertising, appearing in films such
as *The African Queen* and *The Maltese Falcon*.
The gin appears regularly as a named ingredient
in vintage cocktail books.

SEE ALSO
Bombay Spirits Company *p33*
Botanical cuts *p35*
Botanical recipe *p36*
Botanicals *p39*
Cardamom *p49*
Flavour profiles *p87*
Ginger *p114*

Grains of paradise *AFRAMOMUM MELEGUETA* |
BOTANICAL

....

Also known as alligator or Guinea peppers,
grains of paradise are small, peppercorn-like
seeds that form inside pods. This spice and gin
botanical is available both as whole seeds or
in ground form. It is part of the ginger family
(Zingiberaceae) and related to cardamom.

The tall, leafy plant that produces grains of paradise is native to West Africa and grows in coastal swamps. When eaten, the seeds have a peppery, citrus quality but, when distilled, produce a menthol-pepper flavour that adds depth to a flavour profile and extends the finish. The essential oils within grains of paradise include gingerol, paradol and shagaol; these give the seeds their characteristic peppery heat. Because of this, the botanical has been used in the past by unscrupulous individuals to adulterate watered-down spirits; the pepper heat makes a liquid seem more alcoholic than it actually is. Although the spice was used regularly during the early Roman Empire, it did not become popular in Europe until the 14th and 15th centuries, when it was used as a substitute for black pepper and to improve the taste of wine. Examples of gins made using grains of paradise include Bombay Sapphire, Monkey 47 and Opihr.

Grapefruit *CITRUS X PARADISI* | BOTANICAL

A naturally occurring citrus hybrid of sweet orange (*Citrus sinensis*) and pomelo (*Citrus maxima*), which is used as a gin botanical. It traces its origins back to the 17th century and the Caribbean island of Barbados. The hybrid was nicknamed the "forbidden fruit" and was introduced to the American state of Florida in 1823; the first shipments farther north to New York and Philadelphia came in 1885. A series of crossbred and hybrid grapefruits was cultivated in the USA and led to the creation of the pink grapefruit in 1906, followed by the Ruby Red, which was patented in Texas in 1929. The grapefruit has a light, zesty sweetness, which is accompanied by a deeper, lingering bitter note. The fruit is a popular breakfast food and is also

SEE ALSO
Citrus *p58*
Limonene *p148*
Linalool *p150*
Pinene *p177*
Pomelo *p181*
Sweet orange *p216*

juiced for soft drinks. The major producers of grapefruit include China, the United States and Mexico.

The chemical components of the essential oil in grapefruit include alpha-pinene, sabinene, myrcene, limonene, linalool and citronellal, among others. In gin production, the peels of both white and pink grapefruits are commonly used. White grapefruit peel adds a zesty dryness, while pink grapefruit peel typically adds a complex zestiness with a more bittersweet floral note. Examples of gins made using grapefruit as a botanical include Beefeater Crown Jewel, East London Liquor Company Batch 1 Gin, and Sacred Pink Grapefruit Gin.

Green Chartreuse | COCKTAIL INGREDIENT

SEE ALSO
ABV *p13*
Botanicals *p39*
Maceration *p155*
The Last Word *p222*

Green Chartreuse is a key ingredient in various gin cocktails, including the Last Word and the Bijou. A herbal liqueur bottled at 55% ABV, it is made from a selection of 130 botanicals, including various herbs, spices, leaves, seeds and roots. Following the maceration of botanicals and distillation, the distillate is infused with a further selection of plants; it is this final process that gives the drink its distinctive green colour. In 1605, the monks at a Chartreuse monastery in Vauvert, France, received a recipe for an "elixir of long life" from François-Annibal d'Estrées. The manuscript was complex and it was only in 1737 at the Grande Chartreuse monastery in Grenoble, that a monk formed it into a practical recipe. In 1764, the recipe was again adapted to create the liqueur that would ultimately become Green Chartreuse. A sister liqueur, Yellow Chartreuse, was created in 1838. It is bottled at 40% ABV, has a less intense, sweeter character and is coloured with saffron. Although the monks have an eventful history, including having to leave France following the French Revolution, they retained the recipes for their liqueurs and their manufacture moved to the town of Voiron, France, in 1935. The monks continue to produce them today and the liqueur sales fund the running of the monastery.

Greenall's | BRAND

A British gin brand that traces its history back to Warrington, Cheshire, in 1761. They produce a London dry gin, bottled at 37.5% ABV, using Thomas Dakin's recipe from 1761. Botanicals include juniper, coriander, lemon peel, cassia bark, angelica root and ground bitter almonds. The company that owns Greenall's, G&J Distillers, bought the distillery in 1870 and expanded operations during the early 20th century. They are an established contract distillers and produce own-label gin for a number of supermarkets. They also produced gin for The Bombay Spirits Company until 2014. The distillery underwent a renovation that was completed in 2017. In addition to their flagship gin, Greenall's produce, under their own brand, a sloe gin, Greenall's Wild Berry (flavoured with blackberries and raspberries) and Greenall's Extra Reserve (with more of a citrus flavour profile, using the addition of orange and grapefruit to the botanical recipe). Greenall's also own and produce the premium gin brands of Bloom, Berkeley Square, Opihr and Thomas Dakin.

SEE ALSO

ABV *p13*
Almond *p15*
Angelica root *p19*
Bombay Spirits Company *p33*
Botanical recipe *p36*
Cassia bark *p50*
Citrus *p58*
Contract distillers *p67*
Coriander seed *p68*
Fruit gin *p92*
Gin house *p107*
Juniper (common) *p137*
Lemon *p143*
London gin *p151*
Sloe gin *p208*

Hendrick's | BRAND

One of the new wave of gin brands, produced in Scotland since 1999 and owned by whisky producer William Grant & Sons. It has an apothecary-style, dark brown glass bottle and a distinctive flavour profile as they add essences of rose and cucumber after distillation (as such it is not a London dry gin). These are added to their base gin, which has a botanical recipe including juniper, coriander, angelica root, orris root, lemon peel, orange peel, cubeb berries, caraway seeds, elderflower, chamomile and yarrow. The gin's traditional botanicals are distilled in a pot still while the lighter, more delicate botanicals are distilled in a Carterhead still. Hendrick's have successfully marketed their gin using the concept of British eccentricity and encourage drinkers to pair their gin with a fresh cucumber garnish. The gin is available internationally at a variety of strengths: 41.4% ABV in the United Kingdom and 44% ABV in Europe and the United States. In 2017, Hendrick's released Hendrick's Orbium, a quininated gin with additional extracts of wormwood and blue lotus blossom.

Herbal | FLAVOUR PROFILE

Gins with a herbal flavour profile have lots of leafy and herbaceous notes. This could be

SEE ALSO

ABV p13

Angelica root p19

Botanical recipe p36

Botanicals p39

Caraway p46

Carter head still p50

Chamomile p53

Contemporary gin p65

Coriander seed p68

Cubeb berries p73

Cucumber p74

Elder p81

Garnishes p93

Juniper (common) p137

Lemon p143

London gin p151

Orris root p174

Pot distillation p182

Quininated gin p185

Rose p192

Sweet orange p216

Wormwood p239

SEE ALSO

Alpine gin p16

Botanicals p39

Flavour profiles p87

Gin & Tonic *p104*
Martini *p159*
Mint *p164*
Negroni *p168*
Rosemary *p192*
Sage *p197*
Spicy *p212*

H

SEE ALSO
ABV *p13*
Aged gin *p15*
Black peppercorn *p29*
Botanicals *p39*
Cassia bark *p50*
Coriander seed *p68*
Fruit gin *p 92*
Juniper (common) *p137*
Juniper (other species) *p138*
Lemon *p143*
London gin *p151*
Meadowsweet *p163*
Navy strength gin *p167*
Old Tom gin *p171*
Sipping gin *p207*
Sloe gin *p208*
Terroir *p221*
Vanilla *p234*

from the use of fresh or dried herbs as botanicals, with typical examples including rosemary, basil, mint and sage. They often tend to be more resinous in flavour, with notes of pine, spruce or cedar. These gins are usually quite intense and are particularly popular in Alpine countries and central Europe. Like spicy gins, herbal gins work exceedingly well alongside the strong flavours of a Negroni. They also work well in pre-dinner drinks such as the Martini or Gin & Tonic. Examples of herbal gins include Boodles, St George Terroir, Berkeley Square and Gin Mare.

Hernö | BRAND

A distillery and award-winning gin producer located in the village of Dala, close to the City of Härnösand in Ångermanland, Sweden. The distillery was founded in 2011 by Jon Hillgren. The first Hernö product, a London dry gin, was launched on 1 December 2012 using juniper, coriander seed, lemon peel, lingon berries, meadowsweet, black pepper, cassia and fresh vanilla as botanicals. Since opening, Hernö have won an array of awards at international competitions, including the Contemporary Gin Trophy in 2015, Gin & Tonic Trophy, and Gin Producer of the year in 2016 at the International Wine and Spirits Competition (IWSC), as well as a large selection of gold medals from other competitions, including a Double Gold at the San Francisco World Spirits Competition. Other products in the Hernö range include a navy strength gin (bottled at 57% ABV), an Old Tom gin, High Coast Terroir Gin and Hernö Juniper Cask Gin, a gin aged in a barrel made from juniper wood.

SEE ALSO
Base spirit *p21*
Botanicals *p39*
Genever *p94*
Ginniver *p119*
Juniper (common) *p137*
Old Tom gin *p171*

Hollands gin | GIN STYLE

Popular in the middle of the 19th century, Hollands gin is one of the three gins called for in *The Bar-Tender's Guide or How to Mix Drinks* by Jerry Thomas (1862), the other two being dry gin and Old Tom gin. Hollands gin is closely related to Dutch Genever, but is a style of gin in its own right. Like Genever, Hollands gin contains a reasonable amount of malt wine as a spirit base, in addition to the neutral spirit base that is also used in dry gin. Unlike both dry gin and Genever, the range of botanicals used to flavour Hollands gin was historically limited, with distillers often using just juniper or juniper and one or two botanicals, one of which would often be a kind of hop. After the Second World War, popular tastes turned to drier drinks, and the sweeter and maltier flavours of Old Tom and Hollands gin fell out of fashion. Hollands gin was resurrected in 2013 when New York Distilling of Brooklyn, New York, worked with drinks historian David Wondrich to create a New-Netherland Gin, which is a Hollands gin made using a rye whiskey base, juniper and cluster hops. In 2017, Golden Moon and That Boutique-y Gin Company released Frontier Gin, a gin based on an 18th-century recipe for a Hollands gin.

SEE ALSO
Base spirit *p21*
Botanicals *p39*
Old Tom gin *p171*
Terroir *p221*

Honey | BOTANICAL

In gin production, honey is sometimes added to distillation runs to improve the mouthfeel of the gin; it also adds a slightly floral and sometimes woody sweetness. Honey will often take on the characteristics of the surrounding flora, for example pine blossom or orange blossom, which is a useful complement for gin making as many of these plants are also used as botanicals. As honey can be made in urban environments, it is an obvious choice for distilleries that want to add some terroir to their gin. Examples include Dodd's Gin, who use London honey, and Queen's Courage Old Tom Gin that uses New York honey. Honey can also be fermented into mead, which can then be turned into a base spirit from which to make gin. Such is the case with the New York gin, Comb 9. Some gins add honey post-distillation to add flavour, such as Barr Hill Gin. It is also used as a sweetener for some Old Tom gins.

Hybrid gin | GIN STYLE

This refers to a gin that is combined with other spirits. It is usually produced because the distillery wishes to introduce some spirit that was distilled in-house to enhance the gin's flavour, but there are some guidelines that must be followed. In the European Union (EU), the base spirit for gin must have been distilled to at least 96% ABV. If the distillery cannot do this due to the limitations of their equipment, or if the desired flavour of the base material would be stripped out by distilling to 96% ABV, they could not use their in-house base spirit and legally call the final product gin within the EU. Also, the cost of producing the distillate for all of the gin's base spirit in-house would be prohibitive. One example of a hybrid gin is Jinzu, made using Neutral Grain Spirit (NGS) and the following botanicals: juniper, coriander, angelica, yuzu and cherry blossom. After distillation, distilled sake is added. It is worth noting that if the sake had been distilled to 96% ABV, as it is grain-based, the difference between it and NGS would be negligible; distilling sake to this high ABV would strip out most of the flavours. Another

SEE ALSO
ABV p13
Angelica root p19
Base spirit p21
Botanicals p39

example of a hybrid gin is Ginabelle, a Spanish gin that has the distillate of the mirabelle plum added post-distillation. Using this distillate as the base spirit would be both expensive and could overpower the gin's flavour.

I

SEE ALSO
Bramble *p39*
Gin & Tonic *p104*
Shaken/Shaking *p201*

Ice | COCKTAIL INGREDIENT

A crucial ingredient in almost all gin drinks,
ice is water in its solid state. When placed into
a drink, ice has a cooling effect, primarily as a
result of absorbing heat energy from the drink as
it changes from a solid (ice) into a liquid (water);
in short, it cools as it melts. The cooling effect
of radiation from the ice is much lower, which
is why reusable ice cubes are not as effective at
keeping a drink cool as real ice. The presence of
a lot of ice in a glass will help to keep the drink
cooler for longer, delaying melting and dilution.
A Gin & Tonic with a single ice cube is a fast-track
to a warm, watery drink. When shaking a gin
drink with ice, the ice cubes will hit one another
and small shards will break off and melt, thus
cooling and diluting the drink. The ice used
in long drinks is usually in the form of cubes,
produced using trays or purchased in bags.
Cracked or crushed ice consists of small shards
of ice. Given that these melt quickly due to their
smaller size and greater ratio of surface area to
volume, they are less suitable for use in shaken
or long drinks. They are best reserved for drinks
served frappe, such as the Bramble.

J

SEE ALSO
Botanicals *p39*
British juniper *p40*
Juniper (other species) *p138*
Limonene *p148*
Pinene *p177*

Juniper (common) *JUNIPERUS COMMUNIS* |

BOTANICAL

Common juniper is a conifer which provides the one essential ingredient of gin: juniper berries. Without them, a spirit just isn't gin. Indeed, within the European Union, regulation states that for a spirit to be labelled as "gin", it must be made using at least some of the species *Juniperus communis*. The berries are not actually berries, but fleshy seed cones and provide gin with its green, piney and resinous flavour. A member of the Cupressaceae family, juniper trees or shrubs take three or four years to grow to maturity, followed by a further two or three years before the berries are ready to be harvested. The plant is native to the United Kingdom and most of continental Europe, and is found growing across the northern hemisphere. Common juniper has been used since the time of the Ancient Romans and Greeks, when it had a variety of medicinal uses, including treating toothache and headaches. It was also used to aid digestion. Common juniper was one of the many spices used to ward off the Black Death in the 14th century. "Plague doctors" wore masks with long beaks full of juniper berries and other botanicals; they believed that these masked unpleasant smells and stopped the spread of the disease. It worked to a degree, not because the disease spread through the air, but because it was spread by fleas and juniper is an effective, natural flea repellent. In gin production, the ripe, purple berries of juniper are used, typically whole, but sometimes they are milled or gently crushed to release more oils. Chemical compounds contained within common juniper include alpha- and beta-pinene, sabinene, limonene and myrcene.

Juniper (other species) *JUNIPERUS SP.* |

BOTANICAL

In addition to common juniper, there is a small selection of other species that can be used in gin. However, in order to be labelled and sold as "gin" within the European Union, the distiller must use at least some *Juniperus communis*. Alligator juniper (*Juniperus deppeana*) is also known as checkerbark juniper due to the plant's distinctive bark, which has a checkered pattern similar to alligator skin. This variety is native to North America, in particular central and northern Mexico and the southwest of the United States, including states such as Texas, Arizona and New Mexico. When distilled as a gin botanical, alligator juniper has a sappy, cedar nose and a very oily, green, vegetal flavour with cedar and pine notes. Alligator juniper is used in District Distilling Company's Checkerbark Gin. Pinchot juniper (*Juniperus pinchotii*) is also known as red berry juniper due to the orange-red colour of the seed cones (berries). This variety is named after the first Chief of the United States Forest Service, Gifford Pinchot. This juniper is native to northern and central Texas and parts of Mexico. When used in gin, Pinchot juniper provides jammy, floral aromas and a mix of woody pepper and sweet baking spice notes on the palate.

SEE ALSO
Botanicals *p39*
Classic/Juniper-forward *p58*
Juniper (common) *p137*

Ashe juniper (*Juniperus ashei*) is also known as blueberry juniper and post or mountain cedar. This variety is much taller than common juniper, growing up to 15m (50ft) tall. It is native to Texas, Oklahoma, Arkansas and Missouri, and also grows in parts of northern Mexico. The wood is often used to make fence posts and telegraph and telephone poles, hence the name post cedar. In gin, Ashe juniper is extremely piney with lots of woody, resinous notes typical of juniper. It is clean and crisp, but very strong and so should only be used sparingly.

Western juniper (*Juniperus occidentalis*) is also known as sierra juniper; this is the tallest of all varieties of juniper species, growing up to 28m (92ft) in height. The trees are native to the western mountains of the United States, including the states of California, Nevada, Oregon, Idaho and Washington. The trees grow at high altitudes up to 3,000m (10,000ft) in elevation. The Bennett juniper, the largest juniper tree in the USA with a diameter of 3.8m (12½ft), is a specimen of *Juniperus occidentalis*. It is located within the Stanislaus National Forest in northern California. It is estimated to be more than three thousand years old. When used in gin, distilled western juniper has a light hint of pine and tropical fruit, as well as creamy vanilla-oak and cinnamon spice notes. It is quite light and easily overpowered. Cascade Mountain gin uses *Juniperus occidentalis* as its primary juniper variety, but the gin is flavoured through infusion rather than distillation.

Juniper-forward | FLAVOUR PROFILE

See "Classic/Juniper-forward".

SEE ALSO
Botanical recipe *p36*
Botanicals *p39*
Gin Rickey *p111*
Lime (Persian) *p148*
Makrut lime *p156*
Rangpur lime *p187*

Key lime *CITRUS X AURANTIIFOLIA* | BOTANICAL

Also known as the West Indian, Mexican or bartenders' lime, Key lime is used as a botanical in gin production. The fruit is smaller and rounder than the Persian lime, the rind is thinner and more aromatic, and the fruit itself is more acidic. The plant is native to Southeast Asia, where it is a natural hybrid of the biasong (*Citrus micrantha*) and citron (*Citrus medica*). The fruit was introduced to the Mediterranean via the Middle East, before being exported for cultivation in the Caribbean, Florida and the Americas. Today, the Key lime is largely grown in the USA (California, Florida and Texas), in Mexico and Central and South America. When used in distilling gin, the peel is more intense and dryer than that of Persian lime, with less of a floral quality. As such, it can be used more sparingly. Key limes have a wider use in drinks such as the Mojito, Daiquiri and Rickey, and are the key ingredient in a Key lime pie. An example of a gin using Key lime as a botanical is Chilgrove Dry Gin.

K
141

Lavender *LAVANDULA ANGUSTIFOLIA* | BOTANICAL

SEE ALSO
Botanicals *p39*
Flavour profiles *p87*
Floral *p87*
Signature botanical gin *p202*

Lavenders are flowering plants and members of the Lamiaceae family, alongside mint and basil. The most common form of lavender is English lavender (*Lavandula angustifolia*), which despite the name, is native to the Mediterranean countries of Spain, France and Italy. Lavender flowers are often dried and used in herbal medicine and teas. Lavender is also used in a variety of food and drink, such as cakes, biscuits and desserts, as well as soft drinks. In distilling gin, lavender is used in small quantities due to its high oil content and strong flavour. It adds a fragrant floral note with a hint of pine resin which, in balanced amounts, is a great accompaniment to gin. In some instances, lavender is used in post-distillation infusions or as the flavour of a signature botanical gin. Gins using lavender as a botanical include Campfire Gin, East London Liquor Company Premium Gin Batch No. 2 and FEW American Gin.

Lemon *CITRUS X LIMON* | BOTANICAL

SEE ALSO
Bitter orange *p26*
Botanicals *p39*
Garnishes *p93*
Gin & Tonic *p104*
Lime (Persian) *p148*

The most important and popular citrus botanical, not just because of its use in making gin, but because it is also a common garnish choice and key ingredient in many cocktails. The lemon is a hybrid of bitter orange (*Citrus* x *aurantium*) and citron (*Citrus medica*) and likely originated from northeast India or China. Most lemons commonly available at grocers and supermarkets are the Eureka lemon, which has been cultivated so that it flowers throughout the year. Today, lemons are grown in Italy and across the Mediterranean region after being introduced there nearly two thousand years ago. There are also lemon groves in Florida and California in the United States. The juice of the lemon is tart and contains around five percent citric acid. It is commonly used to flavour food and soft drinks, as well as gin cocktails such as the Aviation and White Lady. The peel is full of pockets of essential oil and it is this oil that makes its way into gin during the process of distillation. Between the peel and the flesh of the fruit is a thin layer of white pith, which is bitter and, if used to make gin, adds a somewhat unpleasant flavour. Wedges or wheels of lemon are a common garnish for Gin & Tonics, especially in the UK.

SEE ALSO
Bombay Spirits Company *p33*
Botanical recipe *p36*
Botanicals *p39*
Citrus *p58*
Ginger *p114*

Lemongrass *CYMBOPOGON CITRATUS* | BOTANICAL

Also known as cymbopogon or oil grass, lemongrass is a member of the grass family and is native to South and Southeast Asia. It is classified as a herb and is often sold as a fleshy stalk. It is commonly used in Asian cuisine and is often paired with chicken. It imparts a lemony and lightly fragrant, spiced flavour. Lemongrass is a popular flavour in drinks, where it is often combined with ginger. It is used in various soft drinks as well as tonic waters and herbal teas. Lemongrass contains chemical compounds such as citral, myrcene, citronellal and citronellol. In gin, lemongrass is used as both a distilled botanical and a botanical introduced by post-distillation infusion, such as in Butler's Gin.

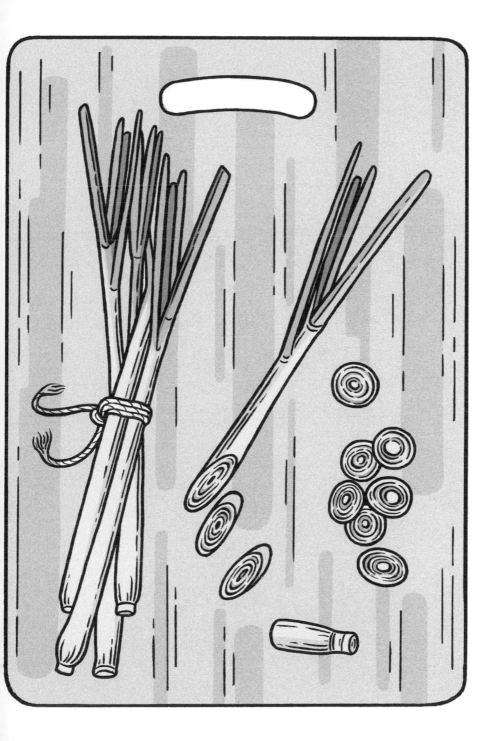

Lemongrass adds a light lemony citrus note, combined with a ginger-like spice and light, aromatic floral quality. It adds a complexity that works well with other citrus and spice botanicals. Other examples of gins made using lemongrass include Bombay Sapphire East and Le Tribute.

Licorice root *GLYCYRRHIZA GLABRA* | BOTANICAL

SEE ALSO
Botanical recipe *p36*
Botanicals *p39*
Old Tom gin *p171*

A plant from the pea and bean family, native to Eurasia, North Africa and Asia Pacific, used as a gin botanical. Today, it is grown in Russia, Spain and the Middle East. The underground stems (roots) of the plant are the primary reason for cultivation; these are dried before being used. Licorice root typically comes in chip, powder or whole (stick) form and, once dried, looks a lot like thin twigs. The root contains a compound called glycyrrhizin, which is 30–50 times sweeter than sugar. Licorice is a popular flavouring for sweets and confectionary, where licorice extract is used; this is obtained by boiling licorice root in water. In distilling, licorice is most commonly used in its powdered form. It adds sweetness and a smooth mouthfeel to gin. This botanical is a key ingredient in many botanically sweetened Old Tom gins such as Jensen's Old Tom.

L

Lillet | COCKTAIL INGREDIENT

SEE ALSO
Bitter orange *p26*
Botanicals *p39*
Dry vermouth *p80*
Sweet orange *p216*
Maceration *p155*
Quinine *p185*
Vesper *p237*
Wormwood *p239*

A fortified wine aperitif produced in Bordeaux, France. It was first created in 1872 by Raymond and Paul Lillet. Lillet Blanc (previously known as Kina Lillet) is produced by macerating botanicals in alcohol, including sweet oranges, bitter orange from Haiti and quinine from South America. After the infusion stage, a blend of various wines is added. Finally, the now-fortified wine is stored in barrels for a number of months, which allows the product to mellow. In 1962, Lillet released Lillet Rouge, a red-wine version of the original aperitif. In 2011, Lillet Rosé was launched. The company also sells two Jean de Lillet Reserves, a red and a white variety. While not technically a vermouth because it doesn't contain wormwood, Lillet Blanc is often used as a substitute for one, most famously in the Vesper cocktail from Ian Fleming's *Casino Royale* and in the Corpse Reviver #2.

Lime (Persian) *CITRUS X LATIFOLIA* | BOTANICAL

The lime is a green citrus fruit which is typically smaller and tarter than a lemon and can be used as a botanical to flavour gin. Persian lime (*Citrus* x *latifolia*), also known as a Tahiti lime, is a hybrid of Key lime and lemon. It is the best-selling variety of lime. It is thought to have been originally cultivated in modern-day Iran, before being introduced to the Mediterranean and, by the 18th century, Brazil. In 1824, it was exported to Australia, then Tahiti, California and, by 1883, Florida. The fruit is sweeter and larger than the Mexican Key lime and is commonly used in food and drink. Gins using Persian lime as a botanical include Tarquin's Gin, Gilpin's Westmorland Extra Dry Gin and Bass & Flinders' Soft & Smooth Gin.

Limonene | CHEMICAL COMPOUND

A naturally occurring essential oil commonly found in the peels of citrus fruits. There are two main isomers (chemical compounds): D-limonene and L-limonene. Both forms are insoluble in water, but miscible in alcohol. The most common of the two isomers, D-limonene, has a strong aroma of oranges. While it is possible

SEE ALSO
Botanicals *p39*
Garnishes *p93*
Key lime *p141*
Lemon *p143*
Makrut lime *p156*
Rangpur lime *p187*

L
148

SEE ALSO
Bitter orange *p26*
Cardamom *p49*
Coriander seed *p68*
Grapefruit *p124*
Juniper (common) *p137*
Lemon *p143*
Lime (Persian) *p148*
Mint *p164*
Sweet orange *p216*

to produce it synthetically, natural sources are so cheap and abundant that these are usually used. The isomer is extracted by the use of centrifuge or steam distillation. Sources of D-limonene include lemons, limes, oranges, mandarins and grapefruits. While the juices of the fruits do contain d-limonene, the isomer is most concentrated in the rind. It can also be found in juniper, coriander and cardamom. L-limonene is commonly found in pine trees and has a turpentine-like scent. Like D-limonene, it is a naturally based solvent and is often used in non-toxic cleaning products. Both isomers can also be used as natural insecticides. L-limonene can be found in pine needles and cones, including juniper berries, as well as mint.

Linalool | CHEMICAL COMPOUND

A naturally occurring chemical compound found in more than two hundred species of plant from many different areas around the world. There are two main types: R-linalool has a sweet, floral lavender and candied citrus character, while S-linalool has a woodier, spicier character with a touch of hops. These types of linalool are found in Lamiaceae such as lavender, mint, basil, sage and rosemary, as well as Lauraceae such as cinnamon, cassia, bay laurel and a variety of citrus fruits, in particular lemon and tangerine. It also occurs naturally in tea, coffee, hops, peach, plum and pineapple. One of the most prevalent sources of R-linalool in gin production is coriander seed, with the essential oils of some high-quality varieties comprising at least 60 percent of this single chemical compound. Some gin experts suggest that the soapiness sometimes found in gin is due to the excessive extraction of linalool from this botanical.

SEE ALSO
Botanicals p39
Cassia bark p50
Cinnamon p57
Coriander seed p68
Lavender p143
Lemon p143
Mint p164
Rosemary p192
Sage p197

SEE ALSO
ABV *p13*
Botanical cuts *p35*
London gin *p151*

London cut | PRODUCTION

A term used to describe London gins that are
distilled in one of the 33 districts that make up
Greater London, which are represented by the
London Assembly and Mayor of London. The
term originated from the fact that, although
London is included in the term "London gin",
spirits adhering to that regulation and eligible
to be labelled as such do not have to be made in
London. It should be noted, however, that having
a designation based on where a gin is bottled
is problematic and would exclude a number of
historic and noteworthy brands. The "cut" was at
one time thought to refer to the process of cutting
with water – also known as "proofing". In the
present day, the "cut" refers to the botanical cuts
that a distiller takes when they make a gin, so the
term "London cut" is another way of saying that
the gin is distilled in London. Despite various
attempts to create a co-ordinated approach
to "London cut" among eligible distillers and
brands, the term currently remains something
that individual distilleries use voluntarily.
Current examples include Knockeen Hills,
Ancient Mariner and Beefeater 24.

SEE ALSO
ABV *p13*
Classic gin *p61*
Juniper (common) *p137*
London cut *p151*
Transatlantic gin *p228*

London gin | GIN STYLE

Commonly referred to as London dry gin,
London gin is a legally protected category of
gin, defined by production technique rather
than whether the gin is made in London or not.
The specific rules are laid out in EU regulation
110/2008. The regulation states that London gin
must be made from ethyl alcohol of agricultural
origin (the base spirit must be distilled to at
least 96% ABV so it cannot be produced solely
through use of a pot still). The gin distillate that

is produced as a result of redistilling must not be lower than 70% ABV. The gin must be flavoured with *Juniperus communis* and that juniper should be the "predominant" flavour. Only water or alcohol can be added after distillation, and the minimum alcoholic strength is 37.5% ABV. Unofficially, "London gin" is sometimes used as a way to describe a traditional style of gin.

Long Pedlar | COCKTAIL

See "Bitter lemon".

SEE ALSO
ABV *p13*
Botanicals *p39*
Filtration *p83*
Juniper (common) *p137*
Maceration *p155*

Louching | PRODUCTION

Louching, also known as "spontaneous emulsification", is a reaction that some spirits have when water is added; as a result, the liquid turns opaque and milky or cloudy. It is a key factor in the preparation of absinthe and pastis, which are both traditionally diluted until almost all of the spirit has louched, sometimes leaving a single, thin band of transparent liquid at the top. Louching is caused by the presence of hydrophobic essential oils, which are soluble in alcohol, but not in water. If a gin has an overconcentration of these botanical oils, it may louche. These heavy oils precipitate or "settle out" as the concentration of alcohol is reduced by adding water, turning the liquid cloudy. While it is usually anise oil that causes absinthe, pastis and ouzo to go cloudy, in gin it is more likely to be juniper or citrus oils.

In the world of gin production, there is some discussion as to whether or not louching constitutes a flaw in gin, with some more established and traditional distillers raising an eyebrow at it, and some of the newer entrants being more open to it. There is very limited evidence that the consumer cares either way. Louching can be avoided using a number of techniques: chill filtering the final gin (but this may strip out other flavours and aromas); the addition of neutral spirit after distillation, which helps to reduce the concentration of botanical oils; reduction of the quantity of botanicals used; or reduction of the length of time during which botanicals are macerated.

SEE ALSO
ABV *p13*
Botanical recipe *p36*
Botanicals *p39*
Compounded gin *p64*
Rectification *p187*

Maceration | PRODUCTION

The process of steeping botanicals in alcohol prior to distillation. The time spent macerating helps to draw out the essential oils in the botanicals so that they are easier to capture during the process of distillation. The length of time taken for maceration varies considerably by botanical recipe and distillery – anything from an hour or two up to 36 hours. The duration of the maceration process affects the degree of extraction, but for some botanicals an overly long maceration can also lead to more bitter and less desirable flavours being released. The structural integrity of the botanicals themselves can also break down if left for too long.

There are two types maceration: cold maceration, where the botanicals are added to spirit at room temperature; and hot maceration, also known as digestion, where the alcohol and botanicals are gently heated, usually to 30–40°C (86–104°F), either in a dedicated vessel or in the pot of the still, prior to distillation. The heat helps to extract more of the botanical oils. The alcoholic strength of the spirit used for maceration is another important factor. If the oils in the botanicals are only soluble in alcohol, the higher the ABV of the spirit, the faster the extraction. For botanicals soluble in water, a high ABV can overextract the flavours with a negative impact on the final product. As such, maceration is a process specific to a distiller's botanical recipe and must be undertaken with care.

Makrut lime *CITRUS HYSTRIX* | BOTANICAL

SEE ALSO
Botanical recipe *p36*
Botanicals *p39*
Gin & Tonic *p104*
Key lime *p141*
Lime (Persian) *p148*
Rangpur lime *p187*

Originating in Southeast Asia, this lime is green with a rough, bumpy, almost wart-like exterior. The rind is aromatic with a slight astringency and, while it can be used to flavour gin, it is more common for the leaves of the plant to be used. These are very aromatic and slightly floral in flavour, with aspects of both lemon and lime. The leaves also make a fragrant garnish to a Gin & Tonic. Makrut limes are sometimes known as "kaffir limes", although this term has negative connotations and so is best avoided. Gins featuring makrut lime leaves include Beefeater London Market, Berkeley Square, Ginraw and Wicked Wolf.

Martin Miller's | BRAND

SEE ALSO
ABV *p13*
Aged gin *p15*
Angelica root *p19*
Botanical recipe *p36*
Botanicals *p39*
Cassia bark *p50*
Coriander seed *p68*
Cucumber *p74*
Juniper (common) *p137*
Lemon *p143*
Licorice root *p147*
Lime (Persian) *p148*
Nutmeg *p168*
Orris root *p174*
Sweet orange *p216*

Owned by the Westbourne Spirits Company, this gin was launched in 1999 by Martin Miller, David Bromige and Andreas Versteegh, who initially found their fame writing a series of pricing guides on antiques. The concept behind the gin was created in the summer of 1998, when Miller decided that he was going to create his own gin, one where "time and money was no object". The gin is made at Langley Distillery in Birmingham in the UK using botanicals including juniper, coriander, angelica, orange, lemon, lime, orris, cassia, nutmeg and licorice. The gin distillate is then shipped to Iceland, where it is proofed with Icelandic spring water and cucumber distillate is added. A higher-strength version of the gin, Westbourne

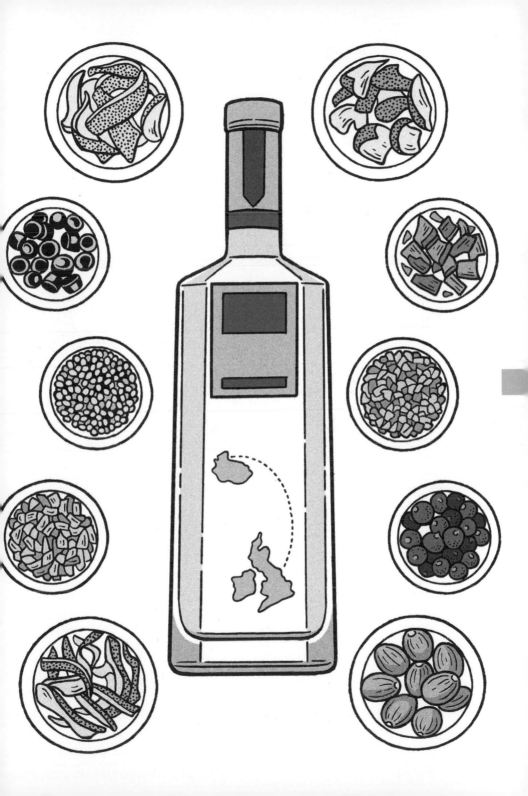

Strength, which has a slight tweak to the original botanical recipe, is bottled at 45.2% ABV. In 2016, Miller's released an aged gin, 9 Moons, which is matured in a single ex-Bourbon cask for nine months.

Martini | COCKTAIL

SEE ALSO
Dirty Martini *p75*
Dry vermouth *p80*
Garnishes *p93*
Glassware *p119*
Ice *p135*
Martini gadgets *p160*

A simple cocktail, but perhaps one of the most controversial; the Martini is a mix of gin and vermouth. The name covers a range of drinks from the Sweet Martini (gin and sweet vermouth), to the Perfect Martini (equal parts gin and dry vermouth), but the most prevalent is the Dry Martini. The origins of the Martini are rooted in those of the Manhattan, which was invented in New York during the 1860s or 1870s. By 1884, a variation on the drink called the Martinez appeared in O H Byron's *The Modern Bartenders Guide*, described as "Same as the Manhattan but you substitute the gin for whisky". In this book, the Manhattan #1 is two parts French (dry) vermouth to one part whisky. Over time, the drink gradually became drier until the first recipe for the Dry Martini was published in the early 20th century. At the same time, Martini and Rossi, a brand of vermouth, was gaining in popularity and so it seems likely that the brand name became attached to the drink that called for it. Turn-of-the-century advertising from Martini and Rossi talks of it being the Martini vermouth for the Martini cocktail. As tastes changed, the Martini cocktail grew progressively more dry, to the point that, by the 1940s, it was not uncommon for people to simply rinse the glass with vermouth or even to merely bow in the direction of France; such was the case in the legend of how Winston Churchill enjoyed his Martinis.

M

159

Most Martinis are served "straight-up" (without ice), but during the 1950s it became popular to drink "Martini-on-the-Rocks", where the ingredients were added along with ice to a tumbler glass and served. While this serving is unusual in the 21st century, it is still popular in smaller towns in the American Mid-West.

DRY MARTINI RECIPE

50ML / 2FL OZ / DRY GIN
10ML / ⅓FL OZ / DRY VERMOUTH
OLIVE OR LEMON TWIST, TO GARNISH

Place the ingredients in a mixing glass filled with ice and stir for 30–60 seconds. Strain into a chilled Martini glass and garnish with an olive or lemon twist.

SEE ALSO
Dry vermouth *p80*
Martini *p159*

Martini gadgets | HISTORY

During the cocktail revival of the 1950s and 1960s, a number of innovative gizmos and bar accessories were created. Most were primarily concerned with adding miniscule amounts of dry vermouth to a drink. Examples include the Martini spike, a silver-plated syringe made by Gorham Co. Dry vermouth would be drawn into the syringe and then could be added in small portions to the cocktail. Martini scales consisted of two metal beakers connected by a pivoted bar, like old-fashioned scales. The pivot could be moved, depending on the desired ratio of gin to vermouth. The beakers were then filled with gin and vermouth, and when the scales balanced, you had the measures for the perfect Martini. Martini stones were small chips of stone designed to be soaked in vermouth and stored in the refrigerator. The stones could then be added directly to a cocktail glass of chilled gin. They were made by Podan & Co. in 1963. The Martini tester was an answer to a question that

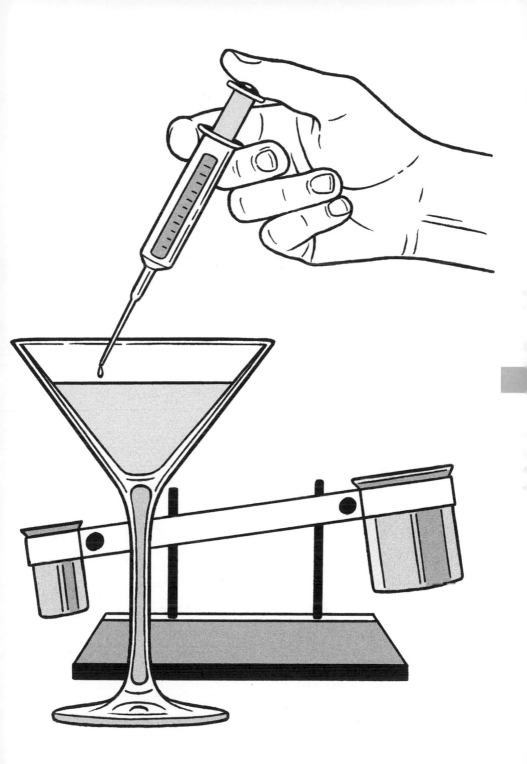

perhaps no one asked: how can I check that the medium-dry Martini I ordered at the bar is really medium-dry? The solution: the Thexton Gourmet Martini Tester. This was a small pipette containing three coloured plastic balls. By sampling the drink, the specific gravity of the drink, as illustrated by the configuration of the balls, identified it as regular, dry or extra dry.

Maturation | PRODUCTION

See "Aged gin".

SEE ALSO
Botanical recipe p36
Botanicals p39
Hendrick's p127

Meadowsweet *FILIPENDULA ULMARIA* | BOTANICAL

Also known as bridewort or lady of the meadow, meadowsweet is a flowering herb in the same family as rose, rosaceae, and can be used as a gin botanical. It is native to Europe and western Asia, but has also been introduced and now grows wild in North America. In Sweden, meadowsweet is commonly used as an ingredient to flavour vodka or other spirits. The alcohol is usually infused with the flowers, which give the liquid their aroma and flavour, as well as giving it a light straw colour. The flavour is lightly sweet, with hay and grass notes, and is somewhat reminiscent of the bison-grass vodkas of Eastern Europe such as Żubrówka. Historically in the UK, meadowsweet was used at weddings; it was often a part of bridal garlands and was thrown over the bride and groom as a precursor to confetti. In gin production, it is used as a botanical in products such as Hendrick's, The Botanist and Hernö. In 2010 Hendrick's replaced the meadowsweet in their botanical recipe with yarrow, as meadowsweet was removed from the "generally recognized as safe list" by the Food and Drug Administration of the United States.

SEE ALSO
Botanical recipe *p36*
Botanicals *p39*
Flavour profiles *p87*
Maceration *p155*
Peppermint *p177*
Spearmint *p221*

Mint *MENTHA SP.* | BOTANICAL

A collection of aromatic plants in the Lamiaceae family, several of which are used as gin botanicals. In addition to the commonly used peppermint and spearmint, other types of mint used in gin production include apple mint (*Mentha suaveolens*) and water mint (*Mentha aquatica*). When distilling mint leaves to make gin, the botanical adds an aromatic leafiness and slight coolness of flavour. It needs to be used sparingly, as mint can easily overpower the gin's flavour profile. Fresh leaves are susceptible to being cooked and stewed when pot distilled, which releases bitter, vegetal flavours. One way around this is to first steep the mint in alcohol and then filter and distil this mint-infused spirit; this avoids exposing the leaves to heat. Gins using mint as a botanical include The Botanist and Dry Fly Gin.

SEE ALSO
Anethole *p16*
Botanical recipe *p36*
Botanicals *p39*
Bush gin *p43*
Licorice root *p147*

Myrtle *SYZYGIUM, MYRICA, BACKHOUSIA SP.* | BOTANICAL

Also known as myrtus, these flowering shrubs belong to the Myrtaceae family and grow around the world. They add a grassy, woody flavour with a little green bitterness when used in gin production. Several myrtles are used. Anise myrtle (*Syzygium anisatum*) is a tall tree that grows in the rainforests of the subtropical regions of New South Wales, Australia. The leaves have a strong character of aniseed due to the presence of the organic compound anethole, which is also found in anise, licorice and fennel. When used as a gin botanical, this adds a sweet, licorice-like flavour. Bog myrtle (*Myrica gale*), also known as sweetgale, is a small shrub that grows in wet peat-like soil. During the 11th century, before the introduction of hops, it was often added to beer to add bitterness. Cinnamon myrtle (*Backhousia myrtifolia*) is a small tree native to the rainforests of subtropical Australia. The leaves have a spicy, cinnamon-like aroma. It is often used in baked goods and desserts. Lemon myrtle (*Backhousia citriodora*) is native to Australia, in particular New South Wales and southern Queensland. It has small, feathery flowers. The leaves are used for various food and drink applications, both in their fresh or dried form. In gin, lemon myrtle adds a leafy citrus note with a flavour reminiscent of a cross between lemon and lime.

M

SEE ALSO
ABV *p13*
Botanical recipe *p36*
Botanicals *p39*
Burrough's *p42*
Plymouth Gin *p178*

Navy strength gin | GIN STYLE

Any gin bottled at 100% old British proof
(57.15% ABV), although – for practicality –
anything between 57% and 58% ABV could be
considered to be navy strength or navy gin.
The alcoholic strength is the only criterion
against which a gin is judged to be navy strength
or not. To create a navy strength gin, some
distillers simply bottle their flagship gin at
a higher strength, by adding less water after
distillation. Others use a unique or modified
botanical recipe to produce a different flavour
profile. In the latter scenario, juniper and
citrus are often increased, and earthy floral
notes reduced. Navy strength gin not only has
a greater intensity of alcohol, but also has a
greater concentration of botanicals, making
for a more intense flavour. Navy gin originated
in the Blackfriars Distillery in Plymouth,
where they started producing a 100% proof
gin for the Royal Navy in the 1850s. By 1855,
the distillery was producing more than a
thousand barrels of Navy gin per year. Between
1863 and the 1950s, Burrough's Distillery
produced another navy gin, Senior Service,
for naval officers, in Deptford, London.

SEE ALSO
Campari *p45*
Ice *p135*
Red vermouth *p191*

Negroni | COCKTAIL

An aperitif cocktail that is bright red in colour and consists of equal parts of gin, red vermouth and Campari. The exact origins of the drink are uncertain, although there are two main versions of the story. The most commonly accepted places the creation at a café in Florence when Count Camillo Negroni ordered a slight variation on the Americano, a mix of red vermouth, Campari and soda water. The Count is said to have been drinking an Americano when, in pursuit of a stronger drink, requested the soda water be replaced with gin. The Count was a dapper man about town and the drink soon became fashionable with the social elite around the world. An alternative story dates the drink back to around 1891 and General Pascal Olivier Count de Negroni. It was said to have been invented by the General as a cure for digestive issues. He mixed it in an Officer's Club and the drink caught on with officers because of its flavour. It then spread around the world. A popular variation of the Negroni is the Boulevardier, which replaces the gin with Bourbon whiskey.

NEGRONI RECIPE

25ML / ¾FL OZ / DRY GIN
25ML / ¾FL OZ / RED VERMOUTH
25ML / ¾FL OZ / CAMPARI

*Fill a tumbler with ice, add the ingredients and stir.
It is best to put the gin in first, otherwise it has a tendency
to float on top of the cocktail, even when lightly stirred.*

SEE ALSO
Botanical recipe *p36*
Botanicals *p39*

Nutmeg *MYRISTICA FRAGRANS* | BOTANICAL

The seed of the nutmeg tree, an evergreen tree native to the Spice Islands (Maluku Islands) in the Pacific, used as a botanical in gin production.

Nutmeg can be used either whole or ground into a powder; the latter method of preparation provides a larger surface area and so the flavour is more easily extracted. Nutmeg gives gin a lightly sweet spiciness and a touch of woodiness. The nutmeg seed is contained inside a red waxy aril (a sort of netting), which is the spice mace. In the 8th century, nutmeg was a highly prized commodity and was worth more than its weight in gold. The earliest recreational recipe for a juniper spirit (gin), dating from 1495, is highly flavoured with nutmeg. In the early 19th century, the British, who were temporarily in control of the Spice Islands, transplanted nutmeg trees to Ceylon, Singapore and Sri Lanka. Nutmeg is also used in a variety of herbal liqueurs such as Drambuie and Bénédictine, as well as to garnish drinks such as Eggnog and the Gin Alexander. Examples of gins using nutmeg as a botanical include Broker's Gin, Oxley Gin and G'vine Floraison.

SEE ALSO
Base spirit *p21*
Botanicals *p39*
Licorice root *p147*
Old Tom gin, Origins of *p173*
Young Tom *p244*

Old Tom gin | GIN STYLE

An old style of botanically intense and sweetened gin that was first mentioned in 1812 in an advert in the *Northampton Mercury*. The style dates from a time before continuous distillation when the base spirit was not as pure and clean as it is today. As such, a strong mix of botanicals and some sugar were added to smooth out the rough spirit. There is evidence of both botanically sweetened and sugar-sweetened Old Tom gins. In an 1802 handbook, the method of sweetening gin is described as adding 35lb of sugar to 130 gallons of gin, which is equivalent to around 1 teaspoon of sugar per 100ml (3½fl oz) of gin. Despite these notes, there is no specific mention of "Old Tom" in the entire book. Botanically sweetened Old Tom gins are sweetened with the addition of naturally sweet botanicals, such as licorice root.

Old Tom gin gained popularity until the invention of continuous distillation, which brought with it an improvement in the quality of base spirit; gin no longer needed to be sweetened. By the 1930s, Old Tom gin became no more than sweetened gin and it disappeared altogether in the late 1960s. The only product that continued to be produced after the 1960s was Golden Cock Old Tom Gin from Norway, which was rarely exported.

In 2007, with the renewed interest in classic cocktails, some distillers resurrected Old Tom gins. The first of these was the British distillery, Hayman's, run by the descendants of Beefeater's James Burrough. This was shortly followed by Jensen's Old Tom Gin, which is botanically sweetened, and Ransom Old Tom Gin from America, which is barrel-aged. Today, there are more than 40 Old Tom gins made at distilleries around the world. Cocktails made using Old Tom gin include the Martinez, Tuxedo and Tom Collins.

Old Tom gin, origins of | HISTORY

SEE ALSO
Gin palace *p111*
Old Tom gin *p171*

There is a number of stories that detail the origins of the term "Old Tom gin". One reference from the 1823 *Slang Dictionary of the Turf* suggests that the name comes from a corruption of "old tun", which was a term for a specific quantity or barrel of gin. An alternative origin story in *Brewers' Phrase and Fable* from 1870 notes, "Old Tom. Thomas Norris, one of the men employed in Messrs Hodges' Distillery opened a gin palace in Great Russell Street, Covent Garden and called the gin concocted by Thomas Chamberlain, one of the firm of Hodges, Old Tom in compliment to his former master." The road was actually Russell Street in Covent Garden and the gin palace was a public house called the Northumberland Arms. All of the key players in this story existed roughly around the time Old Tom must have been created, although there is no evidence that Norris worked with Chamberlain. Another story tells of a cat falling into a vat of gin. This relates to the origin of the logo of one particular gin company, Boord's. Recalled in Boord vs. Huddart in 1903, the plaintiffs recount their inspiration for their logo, which they

O
173

started using in 1849. They even mention having been mocked at the time for using a cat and barrel on their bottles. The book *Life and Unusual Adventures of Captain Dudley Bradstreet*, published in 1775, is often incorrectly cited as the origin of the name. Given that neither the term "Old Tom gin" nor "Tom gin" appears in the text, it is impossible for this to be the source.

Orange *CITRUS SINENSIS* | BOTANICAL

See "Bitter orange, "Sweet orange".

Orris root *IRIS 'FLORENTINA'* | BOTANICAL

SEE ALSO
Botanicals *p39*
Fixatives *p84*
Martin Miller's *p156*

Generally considered as the collective term for the dried and powdered roots of *Iris germanica*, *Iris pallida* and *Iris florentina*, all flowering plants from the family Iridaceae. In gin, however, it is *Iris 'Florentina'*, or the Florentine Iris, that is of particular interest. Orris root, especially for distilling, is primarily sourced from the south of France, northern Italy and Morocco, although it can grow throughout the Mediterranean. Orris root is rarely used for its flavour in gin production, but it does add an earthy sweetness with notes of violet and raspberry. It is mostly prized for its fixative qualities; orris root helps to reduce the volatility of gin, binding the botanical flavours together and helping the spirit to keep its flavour integrity for longer. Orris root also has a long-established use as a fixative in perfumery. Many gins use orris root as a botanical, but those in which it adds a noticeable character include Martin Miller's Gin.

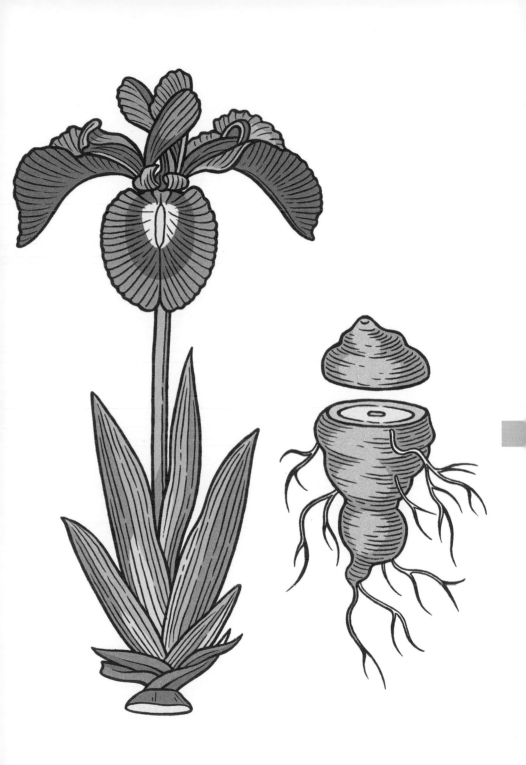

P

SEE ALSO
Botanical recipe *p36*
Botanicals *p39*
Limonene *p148*
Mint *p164*
Pinene *p177*
Spearmint *p221*

Peppermint *MENTHA X PIPERITA* | BOTANICAL

Technically a hybrid of watermint and spearmint, peppermint is native to Europe and the Middle East, and can be used as a botanical in gin production. The leaves are aromatic and used to flavour confectionery, chewing gum and toothpaste, as well as a range of desserts such as ice cream. Peppermint is also used to give scent to cosmetics. For their use in drinks, peppermint leaves are often dried, for example to make peppermint tea. Peppermint is also a key ingredient in the green liqueur, Crème de Menthe and was used to flavour mint gin in the early 20th century. Peppermint contains flavour compounds such as menthol, menthone, menthyl acetate, menthofuran, limonene and pinene. Gins made using peppermint as a botanical include The Botanist and Apostoles, from Argentina.

Pinene | CHEMICAL COMPOUND

Pinene is an organic chemical compound found in some of the botanicals used to make gin. It is one of the contributors to the quintessential aroma and flavour profiles of the spirit. There are two varieties – technically known as structural isomers – of pinene. Alpha-pinene is found in the oils of many conifers such as

SEE ALSO
Botanicals *p39*
Coriander seed *p68*
Juniper (common) *p137*
Lavender *p143*
Lemon *p143*
Mint *p164*
Nutmeg *p168*
Rose *p192*
Rosemary *p192*
Sweet orange *p216*

pine, cedar, spruce, redwoods and fir. It is also present in juniper berries and is a key component that makes gin taste like gin. It is also found in rosemary, eucalyptus and orange peel. Beta-pinene is a colourless liquid that is soluble in alcohol, but not water. This explains why very little flavour is extracted if you try to make tea using hot water and juniper berries. The flavour of beta-pinene is green and resinous with a light, sappy wood note. Beta-pinene is found in many things, including juniper, cumin, hops, coriander, lavender, lemon, orange, mint, nutmeg and rose.

SEE ALSO
Black peppercorn *p29*
Botanicals *p39*
Flavour profiles *p87*
Tonic water *p226*

Pink peppercorn *SCHINUS MOLLE* | BOTANICAL

Also known as pink berry, pink peppercorn can be used as a gin botanical. It is often mistakenly thought to be a member of the Piperaceae family and hence a relation of the black peppercorn, but the pink peppercorn is actually from the Peruvian Mastic tree, sometimes referred to as the Peruvian pepper tree because its berries closely resemble red peppercorns. The plant is native to the dry, arid habitats of northern South America and the Andean deserts of Peru. This peppercorn has a fresh, peppery and aromatic character with a touch of red fruitiness and a little menthol. It is used in small quantities as a botanical to add vigour and complexity to the flavour profile. Also used to flavour a small selection of tonic waters. Gins made using pink peppercorn include Audemus Pink Pepper Gin and Whittaker's Pink Particular.

Plymouth Gin | GIN STYLE

Until 2015, Plymouth Gin had geographically protected status or a geographical indication

(GI). This meant that, to be called Plymouth Gin, the gin had to be made in Plymouth, Devon; it was the only gin in the UK to have this. This was grandfathered in European Union (EU) regulation 110-2008 and seems to have originated from a court case between Plymouth Distillery and a number of other distilleries in London. Plymouth took the London-based firms to court after they released Plymouth gins that were made in the UK's capital. The original Plymouth Gin has been made at the Black Friars Distillery in Plymouth since 1793. The business was started by the firm Fox & Williamson and, by the early 1880s, the distillery was owned by Coates & Co. In 1996, the brand was sold to a group of investors, including John Murphy and Richard Koch. This team hired a new CEO, Charles Rolls, and turned the brand, which had fallen on hard times, around. The brand went from selling around five thousand cases a year to more than eighty thousand, before being sold to V&S Group in 2005, which in turn was sold to Pernod Ricard in 2008. In March 2015, Plymouth Gin's geographical protection expired because they did not renew it. This is likely due to the fact that Plymouth Gin hold the trademark for their name, which outweighs a geographically protected status in EU law.

Pomelo *CITRUS MAXIMA* | BOTANICAL

Also known as shaddock, this is one of the three original citrus fruits, the other two being citrons and mandarins; all other citrus fruits are the result of hybrids of the three types. The pomelo can be used as a botanical in gin production; it is somewhat larger than a grapefruit and the skin ranges in colour from green to yellow, sometimes with a pinkish hue. The pith of pomelo is very

SEE ALSO
Bitter orange *p26*
Botanical recipe *p36*
Botanicals *p39*
Grapefruit *p124*
Sweet orange *p216*

thick. Inside, the flesh is very fibrous and there is a minimal amount of juice. As such, either the whole fruit or the peel tend to be used for food and drink applications. Native to Southeast Asia, the pomelo is one of the parents of the hybrid citruses sweet orange, bitter orange and grapefruit. In gin production, the fresh peel of pomelo is used, partly because dried peel is difficult to come by. The peel adds some of the zestiness associated with grapefruit peel, but with a slight, mellow sweetness. Gins using pomelo as a botanical include Bloom and Monkey 47.

Pot distillation | PRODUCTION

A relatively simple form of distillation undertaken in a vessel containing a mixture of alcohol and botanicals; this vessel is known as the pot, kettle or boiler. Atop this vessel is a sealed, tapered lid known as the head or onion (the latter due to its similarity in shape to an onion). A small pipe known as the swan's neck protrudes from the head, slopes downward, before connecting to the condenser. The condenser is usually a coiled pipe surrounded by a water bath. When making gin, botanicals and base spirit are added to the pot, which is then heated. The alcohol, infused with the essential oils of the botanicals, turns to vapour and passes up through the head and down the swan's neck. Once it reaches the condenser, the vapour is cooled by the surrounding water bath and turns back into a liquid. After the botanical cuts have been taken, the gin rests before being proofed and bottled. The heat used in pot distillation makes it a good choice for those who want to produce bold gins using hardy botanicals that will not break down or become stewed when placed in the still.

SEE ALSO
ABV *p13*
Base spirit *p21*
Botanical cuts *p35*
Botanicals *p39*
Rectification *p187*
Vacuum distillation *p233*
Vapour distillation *p234*

P

SEE ALSO
Bathtub gin *p22*

Prohibition | HISTORY

Also known as the Volstead Act, the National Prohibition Act was an historical federal ban of the production, sale and transportation of alcoholic beverages in the USA. It was enacted to carry out the intent of the 18th Amendment to the US Constitution. Although it was vetoed by then-President Woodrow Wilson, he was overridden by the House of Representatives and the Senate, and the act passed on 28 October 1919. Prohibition officially started on 17 January 1920. There were various socio-economic reasons for the passing of Prohibition, but the primary one was founded in a moral argument, driven by the temperance movement and other religious groups.

Initially, Prohibition was poorly regulated and various criminal organizations became involved in helping drinkers defy the ban by bootlegging, smuggling and running speakeasy establishments. The quality and selection of alcohol was inconsistent, especially with the likes of poor-quality "bathtub gin". This led to a rise in "Prohibition era" cocktails, which tended to include other strong flavours to mask the poor-quality liquor. Prohibition led to the relocation of many of the country's most experienced and influential bartenders. In turn, this led to the spread of cocktail culture, both to the Caribbean and farther afield to cities such as London and Paris. Prohibition ended on 5 December 1933 with the ratification of the 21st Amendment. There were a number of reasons for the repeal, but it was primarily in response to the rise of organized crime that Prohibition had fuelled.

P

183

Proofing | PRODUCTION

See "ABV".

Q

Quininated gin | GIN STYLE

A gin that features quinine or cinchona bark
in addition to other botanicals is sometimes
referred to as quinine or quininated gin.
The first quininated gin, called 1897 Quinine
Gin, was released in 2015 by Atom Supplies,
in partnership with the charity Malaria No
More. Subsequently, quininated gins have
been released by Distillerie de Paris with their
Gin Tonik, and Hendrick's, who released
Orbium in 2017, containing both quinine
and wormwood in addition to the standard
Hendrick's botanicals. Quininated gin is
inspired by the quinine in tonic water and the
idea that, if the quinine was already contained
within a gin, it would be possible to just add
sparkling water in order to produce a drink
similar in style to a Gin & Tonic. This would
avoid the need for tonic water and the additional
sugar that the traditional mix contains.

Quinine *CINCHONA OFFICINALIS* | BOTANICAL

An alkaloid that can be extracted from the bark
of the cinchona tree (*Cinchona officinalis*), which
is native to the Andean forests of the western
South American countries of Peru, Bolivia
and Ecuador. Cinchona bark has been used by
Europeans as a medicinal treatment since the

SEE ALSO
Botanicals *p39*
Gin & Tonic *p104*
Hendrick's *p127*
Quinine *p185*
Tonic water *p226*
Wormwood *p239*

SEE ALSO
Gin & Tonic *p104*
Quininated gin *p185*
Tonic water *p226*

late 16th century. Since the early 17th century, it was found to be an effective treatment for malaria and was used to treat the disease in Rome and the Vatican City. Malaria is caused by a parasite which is spread when a mosquito bites a person and introduces their saliva (containing the parasite) to the human's bloodstream. In the summer, instances of malaria were very common in Rome due to the mosquito-filled swamps surrounding the city. In the 18th and 19th centuries, quinine continued to be used to treat malaria and gradually became a preventative treatment, too. As cinchona bark was very bitter, it needed to be mixed with other ingredients to make it more palatable. One such mix was tonic water.

SEE ALSO
Botanical recipe *p36*
Botanicals *p39*
Key lime *p141*
Lemon *p143*
Lime (Persian) *p148*
Makrut lime *p156*
Tanqueray *p219*

Rangpur lime *CITRUS X LIMONIA* | BOTANICAL

Also known as the lemandarin, the Rangpur lime originated in India. This citrus fruit is a hybrid of a lemon and a mandarin, and has an orange skin. Although often referred to as a lime, it has little relation to other fruits in the group. The juice of the fruit is exceptionally sour with floral honeysuckle notes. Because of this sourness, the Rangpur is sometimes used as a substitute for lime, hence why it is sometimes confused with the green fruit. The leaves of the Rangpur lime are aromatic in a similar way to those of the Makrut lime. It is used as a botanical in Tanqueray Rangpur gin, being added after distillation.

SEE ALSO
ABV *p13*
Botanical cuts *p35*
Botanicals *p39*
Maceration *p155*

Rectification | PRODUCTION

Also known as redistilling, rectification is the process of running alcoholic spirit through a still. There is a variety of reasons for doing this. Firstly, to increase the ABV of the spirit – often used when a fermented mash has been initially distilled to 40–60% ABV to bring it up to a higher strength such as 80% ABV. Or it can be done to "clean up" a spirit by removing some impurities, partly by the taking of heads and tails cuts. Finally, it may be done to add flavour to a spirit by redistilling it with a selection of macerated and un-macerated gin botanicals. Chemically, rectification is essentially the same as distillation, however the term distillation is often reserved for the initial still run, which turns a fermented alcohol liquid into spirit. When issuing distillers' licences, many governments and jurisdictions make a distinction between distillation (the making of alcohol from scratch) and rectification (redistilling alcohol from a third party).

SEE ALSO
Distiller *p76*
Gin house *p107*

Rectifiers' Club | HISTORY

Originally a dining club for distillers, The Rectifiers' Club was founded in the late 18th or early 19th century. Among its members were representatives of all of the classic gin houses, many of whom were related via blood or marriage. At one time, it was once proposed that the Rectifiers' Club was conducting in collusion to fix the prices of spirits and liqueurs, although the evidence suggests that such a cartel, if it existed, was short lived. In the 21st century, the Rectifiers' Club has been revived by a group of individuals with an ardent interest in gin, including retailers, journalists, importers, bartenders and distillers; although this Club appears to be purely social.

SEE ALSO
Glassware *p119*
Ice *p135*

Red Snapper | COCKTAIL

The gin-based version of a Bloody Mary, the Red Snapper is a combination of gin, tomato juice and seasoning, typically including salt, pepper and Worcestershire (or Worcester) sauce. The Bloody Mary, which is made using vodka as its base spirit, was created by Fernand Petiot in 1920. Early recipes for the Red Snapper appeared in the 1940s, but it was not until the 1960s that

it was widely accepted as a gin cocktail. The cocktail is popular at brunches and on airplanes; the latter because of the drink's intense flavour and salinity, which help to compensate for the pressurized and noisy environment of the in-flight cabin. A selection of variations exists for the drink, but the inclusion of olive oil, which gives the drink an elegant silkiness, is known as the Bahmi Old House.

RED SNAPPER RECIPE

50ML / 2FL OZ / GIN
150ML / 5FL OZ / TOMATO JUICE
3–4 LIBERAL DASHES OF WORCESTERSHIRE SAUCE
SALT AND PEPPER, TO TASTE

Fill a glass with ice, add the ingredients and stir.

Red vermouth | COCKTAIL INGREDIENT

SEE ALSO
Botanicals *p39*
Campari *p45*
Dry vermouth *p80*
Martini *p159*
Negroni *p168*
Wormwood *p239*

Also known as sweet or Italian vermouth, red vermouth is a fortified wine flavoured with a variety of botanicals, including wormwood. Despite its name, red vermouth is usually based on white wine and is coloured by infusion or the addition of caramel or another colouring agent. In contrast to dry vermouth, red vermouth has a sweet character, but is also typically more herbal, with deeper, more earthy and slightly bitter flavours. The history of red vermouth goes back to the late 18th century, when the first varieties were produced in Turin, Italy. Red vermouth can be served as an aperitif in its own right or mixed in a wide variety of cocktails such as the Americano, which is made with red vermouth, Campari and soda water. Other classic gin cocktails that call for red vermouth include the Negroni, the Sweet Martini and the Martinez. It is also used in non-gin cocktails such as the Manhattan, Rob Roy and the Boulevardier.

R

191

SEE ALSO
Botanicals *p39*
Carter head still *p50*
Hendrick's *p127*
Hernö *p128*
Pot distillation *p182*

Rose *ROSA SP.* | BOTANICAL

A variety of flowering shrubs from the genus
Rosa, the petals and rosehips from which can be
used to flavour gin. The petals and essential oil
of rose are widely used in perfume and cooking,
especially in desserts and confectionery. Rose
is one of the key flavours of Turkish delight and,
in some countries, including France, rose-
flavoured lemonade is popular. In the United
Kingdom, Fentimans make a variety of rose
lemonade that pairs well with gin. The fruit of
the rose is the rosehip, which is often used to
make herbal tea, but is also used as a botanical in
gin; an example is Crossbill Gin, which is made
using 100 percent Scottish juniper and Scottish
rosehips. Rose petals need to be treated with care
if used in gin production as they are fragile and
the delicate floral notes may not be extracted if
overheated. In fact, it is commonly claimed that
it is impossible to pot distil the flowers. However,
Hernö Swedish Rose is made using distilled
rose petals, which add a floral sweetness to the
gin. A distillate of rose, along with a distillate
of cucumber, is added to Hendrick's Gin, after
the blending of its two initial pot and Carter
head distillates. Another gin made using rose is
Nolet's Silver Dry Gin. Rose is also used to make
rosewater, a cocktail ingredient, and Crème de
Rose, a once-forgotten liqueur that has since
been revived.

SEE ALSO
Botanical recipe *p36*
Botanicals *p39*
Limonene *p148*
Mint *p164*
Pinene *p177*

Rosemary *ROSMARINUS OFFICINALIS* | BOTANICAL

Originating from the Mediterranean with
bright and aromatic leaves, rosemary is a
shrubby evergreen herb with blue, purple or
white flowers, and is a member of the Lamiaceae
or mint family. Rosemary is commonly used

as a culinary herb and seasoning for a range of meats; in the UK, it is regularly paired with lamb. Rosemary leaves are used in both dried and fresh forms, and the dried leaves are also used to make a herbal tea. Rosemary contains flavour compounds such as alpha- and beta-pinenes, carene, camphene, myrcene and limonene. When used as a botanical in gin, rosemary adds an aromatic, leafy and slightly floral flavour and aroma, which really complements resinous juniper notes. Gins made using rosemary include Gin Mare, Boodles and Berkeley Square.

SEE ALSO
Base spirit *p21*
Botanicals *p39*
Pot distillation *p182*
Test still *p222*
Vacuum distillation *p233*

Rotovap | PRODUCTION

Short for rotary evaporator, this is a type of still that uses a reduced pressure system (*see* vacuum distillation page 233). The main vessel holding the mixture of base spirit and botanicals rotates in order to increase the surface area of the contents. This vessel is then gently heated using a water bath; because of the reduced pressure, the distillation will take place at a lower temperature, so botanicals do not need to be exposed to as much heat as in pot distillation. The rotovap is commonly used in chemical research laboratories, but recently has become popular with distillers, bartenders and gourmet chefs. The prototype for the modern rotovap was created by Lyman Craig and was commercialized in 1957 by Büchi of Flawil, Switzerland. Today, most rotovaps are desktop operations, usually around 1 litre (1¾ pints) in capacity, although larger versions – up to 50 litres (88 pints) in volume – are available. The advantages of the rotation of the vessel over normal reduced pressure distilling is that the centrifugal force between the liquid and inside surface of the flask increases the surface area. The centrifugal force, as well as frictional force, also helps to prevent bumping, where the liquid boils over the swan neck of the still.

Royal gin (Geneva) | GIN STYLE

A term used in the late 18th and early 19th centuries to describe the higher-quality varieties of gin. These were produced using whole botanicals rather than oils, tinctures or essences. The following is an example recipe for royal gin:

3LB JUNIPER BERRIES
10 GALLONS PROOF SPIRIT
4 GALLONS WATER

This equates to a charge of around 40% ABV. The mixture would have been distilled and then sold at proof (57.1% ABV). This high-strength gin was the same alcoholic strength as the latter-day navy strength gin. The fact that it was sold at this high strength provided some evidence to consumers that the gin had not been adulterated with sugar or other oils and had been flavoured solely through distillation.

SEE ALSO
ABV *p13*
Botanicals *p39*
Common gin *p64*
Navy strength gin *p167*

R

Saffron *CROCUS SATIVUS* | BOTANICAL

SEE ALSO
Botanical recipe *p36*
Botanicals *p39*

A spice made from the stigmas of a flower called
the saffron or autumn crocus (*Crocus sativus*);
these are dried before use. Weight for weight, it
is the world's most expensive spice. The flower
is native to Southwest Asia, but is also cultivated
in Europe, North Africa, North America and
Oceania. Saffron has a hay-like, spiced character
with a little smokiness. It is used as a distilled
botanical in some gins, but it is more commonly
used in post-distillation. Examples include Old
Raj Gin and Nolet's Reserve Dry Gin. This is
likely due to the expensive nature of the spice and
the fact that more of the flavour comes through
in infusion than distillation. There is also a small
subcategory of infused gins which are described
as "saffron gin". These typically tend to be a
deep orange in colour and have saffron as a very
discernable part of their flavour profile. The first
of these was Gabriel Boudier's Saffron Gin.

Sage *SALVIA OFFICINALIS* | BOTANICAL

SEE ALSO
Botanical recipe *p36*
Botanicals *p39*
Pinene *p177*
Wormwood *p239*

A herb, also known as common or garden sage,
which is a member of the Lamiaceae (mint)
family and native to countries around the
Mediterranean Sea. Sage is a popular seasoning
in cooking across Europe, including the UK,
Italy and the Baltic States. It is a key flavour in

the stuffing that accompanies roast turkey at holidays such as Thanksgiving and Christmas. It is also often paired with pork, either when roasted or processed into sausages. In gin, sage adds a leafy flavour with a hint of pepperiness and herbal complexity. It helps to balance out sweeter and more citrusy notes. Sage contains camphor and alpha-pinene and is also a source of alpha- and beta-thujone. The botanical typically has a higher concentration of the latter chemical compound than wormwood, which is the main source of thujone in absinthe. Gins that features sage as a botanical include Boodles, St George Spirits' Terroir Gin, Gilpin's and Berkeley Square.

Seagram's | BRAND

SEE ALSO
ABV *p13*
Aged gin *p15*
Botanical recipe *p36*
Prohibition *p183*
Sipping gin *p207*
Yellow gin *p243*

A brand of gin popular in the United States of America made using a botanical recipe of juniper, coriander, angelica root, and both bitter and sweet orange. It is bottled at 40% ABV. In 1857, a distillery was founded in Waterloo, Ontario in Canada that Joseph E Seagram took over in 1883, naming the company Joseph E Seagram & Sons. After Seagram's death in 1919, the company merged with Distillers Corporation Limited, owned by Samuel Bronfman. The new company, which kept the Seagram's name, set up business in the United States in the 1930s following the repeal of Prohibition in 1933. They successfully sold aged whiskeys and, in 1939, released the Extra Dry Gin that is popular today, then called "Seagram's Ancient Bottle Distilled Dry Gin". This was matured in white oak casks, which gave it a distinctive pale yellow colour. Early advertisements highlight the mellowing effect that the wood had on the spirit, but – with the exception of some barrel charms added

to the bottles in the 1950s – the aging was not emphasized in the gin's marketing. Its name evolved over the years from "Seagram's Golden Gin" (1950) to "Seagram's Extra Dry Golden Gin" (1955) and then to "Seagram's Extra Dry Gin" (1960). Fifty years later, in 2010, Seagram's stopped barrel-aging their gin, citing a need for greater quality control. The gin kept its traditional flavour profile and its pale yellow colour, although in some markets, such as Spain, the gin is clear. From the 1950s onwards, the company diversified into other markets and by 2000, Edgar Bronfman Jr, descendant of Samuel Bronfman, sold the beverage division of Seagram's to Pernod Ricard and Diageo. In the early 21st century, Seagram's launched a range of flavoured "Twisted Gins", which are bottled at 35% ABV. The fruit flavouring comes from the addition of liqueurs, with flavours such as lime, pineapple and peach.

Shaken/Shaking | MIXOLOGY

SEE ALSO
ABV p13
Ice p135
Stirred/Stirring p215

A method by which a drink is vigorously mixed. Ice is placed into a cocktail shaker, along with the drink's ingredients. The shaker is then sealed and shaken with vigour. Shaking has a number of impacts upon the ingredients. It helps to mix or combine them and cools the ingredients due to ice melt. Also, the alcohol in the drink is slightly diluted when the ice melts. A cocktail that started off at 40% ABV, on average, ends up around 26–30% ABV after shaking with ice. The process of shaking also traps small air bubbles in the liquid, making it appear cloudy and giving the drink a fluffier, softer texture; this is sometimes known as "bruising". A cocktail should be shaken for between 30 and 60 seconds, depending upon the size of the shaker; although the best method for determining when your cocktail is ready is to shake until the outside of the shaker becomes frosted (ice starts to form on the outside). Because some small shards of ice break off the larger cubes during shaking, it is often necessary to fine strain or double strain the drink before serving. This involves the use of a fine mesh strainer, much like those used to filter out the leaves when pouring loose-leaf tea. A dry shake is a different technique, which involves shaking the ingredients together before the addition of ice. Ice is then added and a second shake undertaken. This is commonly used when a cocktail recipe includes pineapple juice or egg whites. The dry shake helps to emulsify the liquid and create a lighter, smoother and frothier texture to the drink.

Signature botanical gin | GIN STYLE

An emerging category of gin that involves a particular flavour being highlighted on the gin's label beyond that of juniper. This particular flavour is known as the signature botanical. As of 2017, the International Wine & Spirits Competition has included Signature Botanical as a recognized gin category. The first modern signature botanical gins were released in the first few years of the 21st century; an example being Knockeen Hills Heather Gin. Like other signature botanical gins, this was an unsweetened gin, produced at the Timbermill Distillery, whose flavour came completely through distillation and so could technically be considered a London gin. This is essentially what separates signature botanical gins from other macerated or fruit gins. Today, signature botanical gins are made around the world, but are particularly popular in Australia, the

SEE ALSO
Botanical recipe *p36*
Botanicals *p39*
Elder *p81*
Fruit gin *p92*
Lemon *p143*
London gin *p151*
Maceration *p155*
Sweet orange *p216*

S

United States, the United Kingdom and Europe. Popular flavours for signature botanical gins include orange, lemon and elderflower. Unlike fruit gins, which are often sweetened, signature botanical gins are dry and can be mixed in a similar way to regular gins.

Signature serve | MIXOLOGY

SEE ALSO
Cucumber *p74*
Garnishes *p93*
Gin & Tonic *p104*
Hendrick's *p127*
Rose *p192*
Seagram's *p198*

The signature serve is a particular combination of ingredients that create a drink which specifically complements the characteristics of the gin. For example, a gin that features rosemary quite heavily may work well when paired with a more herbaceous tonic and garnished with lemon or even lemon thyme. The signature serve exists to give bartenders and consumers an idea of how to mix the drink. It should be visually attractive, taste great and be quick and easy to make with readily obtainable ingredients. The signature serve is not designed to be prescriptive and dictate the only way to mix the gin; rather, it is there to provide inspiration. Another good example of a signature serve is the use of cucumber in a Gin & Tonic made with Hendrick's Gin. The gin contains both rose and cucumber and the pioneering use of a cucumber garnish over lemon or lime really captured the drinking public's imagination. It is worth noting that an advert for Seagram's Gin in the 1970s suggested a cucumber garnish, but it did not take off at that time.

Single Bottle Act | HISTORY

SEE ALSO
Booth's *p34*
Distillery *p79*
Gin house *p107*
Gordon's *p120*
Tanqueray *p219*

Officially described as "An Act for granting to Her Majesty certain Duties of Excise and Stamps", this Act of Parliament was passed in Great Britain on 28 June 1861. It allowed a licenced dealer of spirits to "sell by retail foreign and British spirits". The minimum bottle size for domestic spirits was one quart (1.14 litres/ 2 pints) or, for imported spirits, the same bottle in which the spirit was imported. These spirits were not allowed to be consumed on the premises of the retailer. This act paved the way for the first off-licences or liquor stores. This development came at around the same time as the reputations of the great gin houses or gin brands were becoming established. Prior to this, a gin distillery would simply sell their gin to a publican, who would adulterate it with water or sugar (if patrons were lucky; worse things if they were not). As such, the distilleries did not have control over what their consumers received. Selling gin by the bottle meant that distilleries could seal the containers before shipping them to merchants, who would sell the gin directly to consumers. They could be far more confident that the consumer would taste the gin exactly as the distiller intended. This helped companies such as Booth's, Tanqueray and Gordon's to build reputation and brand loyalty.

Single shot | PRODUCTION

On a fundamental level, gin is made when spirit and botanicals are placed in a pot still and distilled. The resulting distillate is then proofed with water and, after some time for the gin to settle, it is ready to drink. This is referred to as single or one-shot distillation. For example, a distiller users 1kg (2¼lb) of botanicals to create a gin and ends up with 50 litres (11 gallons) of distillate at 80% ABV. This is proofed 50/50 with water to create 100 litres (22 gallons) of gin at 40% ABV. This one distillation run has created 100 litres (22 gallons) of gin.

SEE ALSO
ABV *p13*
Botanicals *p39*
Pot distillation *p182*

If the distiller decides to double the quantity of botanicals to 2kg (4½lb) and keeps everything else the same, he will end up with 50 litres (11 gallons) of distillate at 80% ABV that has double the concentration and intensity of botanical flavour. This means that the distillate can be mixed with 50 litres (11 gallons) of neutral spirit at 80% ABV without losing any of the flavour intensity of the first example. The distiller can then proof these 100 litres (22 gallons) to create 200 litres (44 gallons) at 40% ABV. This second distillation run has created twice as much gin. This is known as the multi-shot, multi-fold or concentrate method of distillation. Some distillers use a 10 or even 20 times concentration, meaning that one distillation run could create up to 2,000 litres (440 gallons) of finished gin using the multi-fold method, compared to only 100 litres (22 gallons) using the single shot method. The primary benefit of the multi-shot method is that it is a more efficient use of a still and allows the distiller to increase production without the need for additional equipment and costly capital expenditure.

Sipping gin | GIN STYLE

A modern style of aged gin, as distinct from yellow gin. The character of sipping gin is determined by achieving a fine balance between the notes of the wood and those of the gin's botanicals. Unlike yellow gins, sipping gins are designed to be drunk on their own or mixed in a similar fashion to whisky, often paired with red vermouth and other herbal or spicy ingredients. Cocktails usually made with sipping gin include the Manhattan, Negroni and the Old Fashioned. Sipping gins are usually aged for months rather than weeks; the average is between three and

SEE ALSO
Aged gin p15
Negroni p168
Red vermouth p191
Yellow gin p243

six months. In the case of Alambic's Special Caribbean Gin, it is aged for 14 years in used whisky casks, then a further two years in used Caribbean rum casks.

Sloe gin | GIN STYLE

SEE ALSO
Bitter lemon *p26*
Plymouth Gin *p178*

A fruit liqueur created by infusing sloe berries in gin and adding sugar or honey to sweeten. Sloe berries are the fruits of the blackthorn bush (*Prunus spinosa*), which is native to Europe and western Asia. The fruit has a dark, plummy, astringent flavour with a little almond nuttiness from the seed. The liqueur is thought to date from 17th-century England when hedgerows, a rich source of sloes, were planted to separate plots of land created by the Enclosure Acts. Sloe gin was a way to preserve the sloe berries, which were too tart to be eaten on their own. The popularity of sloe gin increased during the Gin Craze of the 18th century, when it was described as "poor man's port". In 1803, the Hawker's brand was founded; they eventually produced the Pedlar's brand of sloe gin. Plymouth Gin, made in the same city, released theirs in 1883. The nearby area of Dartmoor was a plentiful supply of sloe berries. The Pedlar brand led to the creation of one of the most famous sloe gin drinks: the Long Pedlar, a mix of sloe gin and bitter lemon. Other cocktails include the Sloe Gin Fizz. Notable brands of sloe gin available today include Plymouth, Sipsmith and Hawker's.

Soda water | COCKTAIL INGREDIENT

SEE ALSO
Bitter lemon *p26*
Tonic water *p226*

Also known as fizzy or carbonated water, club soda or seltzer, soda water is carbon dioxide dissolved in water and was the first carbonated drink. Some naturally carbonated waters have

high amounts of dissolved minerals due to the presence of carbon dioxide; this is usually released from volcanic rocks near the source of the spring. Such waters were historically prized for their health benefits. In 1767, natural philosopher and clergyman Joseph Priestley invented a process for artificially carbonating water by suspending a bowl of water over a beer vat in a Leeds brewery. The carbon dioxide released from the fermenting beer dissolved into the water, carbonating it. At the time, Priestley theorized that it was a possible cure for scurvy. In 1783, Swiss jeweller Jacob Schweppe released a commercial carbonated water. The main difference between carbonated water and club soda is that the latter has additional ingredients such as Himalayan salt to give it a mineral quality. Historically, this was because the carbon dioxide used in the United States was made from a mix of chalk and sulphuric acid, which gave the water an acidic quality; the salt was added to balance the flavour. Soda water is a key ingredient in Gin & Soda and Gin Collins. It was also the precursor to other carbonated drinks such as tonic water, bitter lemon and cola.

Spearmint *MENTHA SPICATA* | BOTANICAL

SEE ALSO
Botanical recipe *p36*
Botanicals *p39*
Limonene *p148*
Mint *p164*
Peppermint *p177*
Pinene *p177*

Also known as common or garden mint, spearmint is native to Europe and Asia, but now grows across the world, including the Americas, North and West Africa, as well as parts of Oceania. The leaves have pointed tips, hence the name "spear" mint. Spearmint leaves are used in a number of popular cocktails, including the Bourbon-based Mint Julep and the rum-based Mojito. Unlike peppermint, spearmint does not contain large quantities of menthol or menthone, but does contain alpha-pinene, beta-pinene, carvone, limonene and eucalyptol. Gins that use spearmint as a botanical include The Botanist and Cardinal from the United States of America.

Spicy | FLAVOUR PROFILE

SEE ALSO
Botanicals *p39*
Cassia bark *p50*
Cinnamon *p57*
Cloves *p62*
Flavour profiles *p87*
Gin & Tonic *p104*
Grains of paradise *p123*
Negroni *p168*
Nutmeg *p168*
Pink peppercorn *p178*

One of the flavour profiles into which gins can be categorized. The spicy flavour profile can be subdivided into sweet spice and savoury spice. Sweet spice has botanical flavours from spices such as nutmeg, cinnamon, cassia and clove; while savoury spice focuses on botanical flavours such as cumin, pepper and grains of paradise. Spicy gins are often praised for their complexity and soft, round mouthfeel. They also help to introduce flavours to gin that a new drinker might not expect. Spicy gins work well in hot drinks and cocktails with strong flavours such the Negroni. They also make great autumnal Gin & Tonics. Examples of sweet spice gins include Portobello Road, Knickerbocker and Edinburgh Gin. Examples of savoury spice gins include Darnley's View Spiced and Audemus Pink Peppercorn Gin. Examples of spicy gins with both sweet and savoury spice are Opihr and Bombay Sapphire East.

Star anise *ILLICIUM VERUM* | BOTANICAL

SEE ALSO
Anethole *p16*
Botanical recipe *p36*
Botanicals *p39*
Louching *p153*

The dried seed pod of the tree *Illicium verum*, an evergreen tree native to Vietnam and southern China, which can be used as a botanical in gin production. The star-shaped pod usually has eight points, each of which contains a shiny, kernel-like seed. Star anise is oily and has a strong, anise-like flavour, although it is not actually related to anise. The similarities in aroma and flavour are because both contain anethole. Star anise has a variety of culinary,

cosmetic and pharmaceutical uses. It is one of the components of Chinese five spice. Star anise is used in the liqueur Galliano and to flavour sambuca, pastis and absinthe. The high oil content of this botanical is the reason why many of these spirits louche. In gin distillation, star anise adds a spicy sweetness. Due to its high oil content and strong flavour, it needs to be used sparingly as it can easily overpower a gin's flavour. Examples of gins using star anise include St George Spirits' Botanivore Gin and Citadelle Gin.

Stirred/Stirring | MIXOLOGY

SEE ALSO
Ice *p135*
Martini *p159*
Shaken/Shaking *p201*

A method of mixing a drink using a mixing glass filled with ice. The ingredients are added to the glass and then stirred with a bar spoon or other implement. In a similar way to shaking, stirring both combines the ingredients and chills and dilutes the drink due to the melting of the ice. Because stirring ingredients mixes them less vigorously than shaking, they do not cool as quickly and no aeration takes place, resulting in a clearer drink than its shaken counterpart. Some Martini aficionados believe that this makes the drink taste more pure.

Strawberry gin | GIN STYLE

SEE ALSO
ABV *p13*
Fruit gin *p92*
Maceration *p155*

A type of gin with the flavour of strawberries. The rise in popularity of strawberry gin began in Valencia, Spain in 2013–14. A local brand, Gin Puerto de Indias, was released and the phenomenal success of this product, which was typically served with Lemon Fanta, caused a number of other Spanish brands to rush similar products to market. By the beginning of 2015, more than 30 products were available. The

S

215

production methods of these gins varied greatly, from the addition of strawberry flavouring and pink colouring to an existing gin, to a more careful infusion of fresh strawberries in dry gin, which is then lightly sweetened. As a result, there is great inconsistency in quality: products range from being little more than a pink strawberry vodka to those that genuinely capture the essence of the aroma and flavour of the fruit alongside the traditional flavours of gin. The strengths of the gins also vary from 37.5–42% ABV. In recent years, the mania surrounding strawberry gin seems to have relaxed a little, although many are still available.

SEE ALSO
Bitter orange *p26*
Botanical recipe *p36*
Botanicals *39*
Pomelo *p181*

Sweet orange *CITRUS SINENSIS* | BOTANICAL

Thought to have originated in southern China, sweet orange is a hybrid of the pomelo (*Citrus maxima*) and the mandarin (*Citrus reticulata*) and is used to flavour many different gins. They were introduced into Spain by the Moors in the 10th century. Sweet orange is often juiced to create orange juice, a popular breakfast drink which is commonly available in filtered and unfiltered varieties. The peel of sweet orange contains essential oils that can be extracted to make orange essence. This essence is used to flavour a variety of sweets and desserts. The petals are also used to create "orange blossom water", a citrus variation of rosewater. Beehives located near orange groves produce a particularly aromatic type of honey that is often sold as "orange blossom honey". In gin production, sweet orange peels are used, either dried or fresh, to add a lightly sweet citrus note, a gentle florality and a juicy mellowness to the spirit. The flowers (orange blossom) are sometimes used alongside citrus peels in gin

production to enhance their flavour and add a light florality. Today, the main producers of sweet oranges are Brazil, followed by the USA and Mexico. Popular varieties include Valencia oranges, Navel oranges, Jaffa oranges, Narinja oranges and blood oranges. Sweet orange is used as a botanical in Beefeater Gin, City of London Distillery Gin and Adnams Copper House Gin.

Sweetening the still | PRODUCTION

A method dating back to the 18th and 19th centuries which is rarely practised in modern days, except among some small distillers. Sweetening the still takes place in a still that is used for making a variety of spirits, most typically a pot still. The distiller will plan out a specific order in which to produce their range of spirits in such a way that some of the character of each spirit will leave some residual flavour in the still, which will be picked up in the flavour profile of the next spirit to be made. For example, a distiller may use their still to make a gin using juniper, caraway and anise and do all of this just before making grappa on the same still. The desire being that some of the essential oils from the gin's resinous, sweet and spicy botanicals will remain in the still and add a subtle, additional complexity to the otherwise unflavoured grape spirit.

SEE ALSO

Botanicals *p39*
Caraway *p46*
Distiller *p76*
Juniper (common) *p137*
Pot distillation *p182*

S

Tanqueray | BRAND

SEE ALSO
ABV *p13*
Angelica root *p19*
Chamomile *p53*
Coriander seed *p68*
Gin house *p107*
Ginger *p114*
Gordon's *p120*
Grapefruit *p124*
Juniper (common) *p137*
Licorice root *p147*
Lime (Persian) *p148*
Rangpur lime *p187*
Sweet orange *p216*

A major gin brand based in the UK and owned by Diageo. The company's largest market is in the United States. Their primary products are a London dry gin (at 43.1% ABV in the UK and 47.3% ABV for export) and a premium gin: Tanqueray No. Ten. The botanical recipe for the London dry includes juniper, angelica root, coriander seed and licorice. Tanqueray No. Ten uses the same botanical recipe, plus chamomile flowers, orange, lime and grapefruit. Other products include Tanqueray Rangpur, which adds rangpur limes, ginger and bay leaves to the original botanical recipe; and Tanqueray Malacca, a slightly sweeter, fruitier variety which was discontinued at the end of the 20th century.

The company was founded by Charles Tanqueray in Bloomsbury, London, in 1830. In 1898, Tanqueray merged with Gordon's, creating Tanqueray, Gordon's & Co., which was later acquired by The Distillers Company. This was later taken over by Guinness & Co. to become United Distillers, which is now a part of Diageo. From the 1950s onwards, Tanqueray was marketed specifically for the export market, gaining notable popularity in the United States. The original Tanqueray distillery was badly damaged during the Second

T
219

World War. Production moved from Essex to Cameron Bridge in Scotland in 1998. Like Gordon's, Tanqueray has a distinctive bottle design in green glass. The crest on the bottle depicts a pineapple, a symbol that historically has represented hospitality and prosperity.

SEE ALSO
Base spirit *p21*
Botanicals *p39*
Yuzu *p245*

Terroir | PRODUCTION

Unlike terroir in wine, terroir in gin is not determined by the exact geological, geographical and environmental conditions surrounding a distillery. Instead, it refers to the way in which a distiller manages to capture the character of an area through their choice of botanicals or, in some cases, base spirit. Botanicals can either be locally sourced or can have a flavour that is either evocative of, or is particularly popular in, a given location. For example, a distillery by the sea may use rock samphire or kelp; a distillery in Seattle may use blackcurrant because it is a popular local flavour; Japanese gin distilleries often use botanicals associated with Japan, such as yuzu or cherry blossom; or distilleries located in or near major vine-producing regions, such as California, New York and Australia, will often use a base spirit made from local grapes. Another way to capture terroir in gin is to use a local water supply, although this is likely to have more impact on a marketing backstory than on the discernable character of the gin. One limitation of using terroir in gin, especially locally sourced botanicals, is that often they will only be available for a season, which makes year-round production problematic. One solution is to limit the terroir gin to a seasonal release. Alternatively, it may be suitable to freeze or dry botanicals, or create a concentrated botanical distillate which can then be stored until needed.

SEE ALSO
Botanical recipe *p36*
Botanicals *p39*
Cardamom *p49*
Lavender *p143*
Pot distillation *p182*
Rotovap *p194*

Test still | PRODUCTION

Also known as a prototype still, this is a still that is much smaller than those used for commercial gin production, typically between 1 and 10 litres (1¾ and 17½ pints) in size. The smaller volume allows the distiller to experiment with new ideas and recipes without having to commit the resources that a full still run would demand. Test stills are generally made of copper or glass and are usually heated by an electric hot plate. In some cases, a distillery may use a rotovap as a test still. Test stills can also be used to create an individual botanical distillate when a distillery is investigating the viability of using a new, unusual botanical. It is worth noting that if a distiller is happy with the results from their test still, caution must be used when scaling the recipe up so that it can be used on a larger production still, as the increase is not necessary a linear one. This is because some botanicals have a disproportionate effect on the character of the gin when distilled in larger quantities. Examples include citrus, cardamom, lavender and anise, among others; these botanicals "push above their weight" and this needs to be compensated for when calculating the botanical recipe for the larger still.

The Last Word | COCKTAIL

A gin cocktail first referenced in Ted Saucier's 1951 drinks book, *Bottom's Up*. According to Saucier, the history of the drink goes back a further 30 years or so to the Detroit Athletic Club, a private social and athletic club in Madison Street, Detroit, Michigan, where the drink had been served from at least 1916. It was either created by, for, or named after, Frank Fogarty,

SEE ALSO
Glassware *p119*
Green Chartreuse *p125*
Ice *p135*
Shaken/Shaking *p201*

a vaudevillian monologist, hence the cocktail's name. Like many drinks from the Golden Era of cocktails, the drink fell out of fashion and was forgotten by the 1960s or 1970s. It was revived by Murray Stenson of the Zig Zag Café in Seattle in 2004.

THE LAST WORD RECIPE

30ML / 1FL OZ / DRY GIN
30ML / 1FL OZ / FRESH LIME JUICE
30ML / 1FL OZ / GREEN CHARTREUSE
30ML / 1FL OZ / MARASCHINO

Place all the ingredients into a cocktail shaker filled with ice, shake well and strain into a Martini or coupe glass. If you prefer a drier drink, double the quantity of gin.

Throwing | MIXOLOGY

SEE ALSO
Ice *p135*
Martini *p159*
Negroni *p168*
Prohibition *p183*

A long-forgotten way of mixing drinks that dates back to the Prohibition era. It involves passing the drink between two cocktail shaker tins (bases) and slowly moving the receiving tin farther away, so that the liquid pours for longer. The mixture becomes oxygenated as it passes through the air, which helps to give the drink a light, fluffy texture. The ice is kept in the first tin with the use of a cocktail strainer. This method was used in the El Floridita Bar in Havana, Cuba, where it was known as "Escandiado". It is still sometimes referred to as "Estillo Cubano" or "Cuban Style". Throwing was learned in El Floridita Bar in the early 20th century by Miguel Boadas, who was born in Havana in 1895. In 1925, Boadas moved to Barcelona, where he opened Boadas Bar in 1953, bringing the art of throwing with him. This location was one of the last few refuges of the technique and it was routinely used for Martinis, Manhattans and Negronis. Some time later, from 2012 onwards, various bartenders and cocktail historians

T

225

endeavoured to reintroduce throwing. The method is similar to that of rolling, which involves passing a mix of ingredients, including ice, between two cocktail shaker tins. There is no long pour involved in rolling and the aim is to get as little aeration as possible.

Tonic syrup | COCKTAIL INGREDIENT

SEE ALSO
Soda water *p208*
Tonic water *p226*

Tonic syrup is the concentrated form of tonic water. It is generally mixed with sparkling water to create tonic water, but can also be used as a cocktail ingredient in its own right. The concept of tonic syrup has been around for decades; the brand SodaStream have sold a tonic syrup for use in their home carbonation machines since the 1970s. Tonic syrup gained in popularity in the United States in 2010. Around this time, bartenders were starting to rediscover old cocktails and techniques, and began to pay attention to using more fresh and homemade ingredients. John's Premium Tonic of Arizona was one of the first varieties commercially available. The choice to sell the syrup in its concentrated form rather than diluted, carbonated and bottled, was largely down to the cost and the environmental impact of shipping cases of bottles across the country. In contrast, Europe, which has established and accessible road networks connecting more than 20 countries, has seemed to prefer ready-mixed tonic waters, and tonic syrup is still a novelty.

Tonic water | COCKTAIL INGREDIENT

SEE ALSO
Gin & Tonic *p104*
Gin Tonica *p113*
Pink peppercorn *p178*
Quinine *p185*
Tonic syrup *p226*

Also known as Indian tonic water, quinine water or quininated water, tonic water is a sparkling soft drink that contains quinine, citric acid and sugar. The concept of combining tonic water

and wines, in particular with supposed health benefits, has been around for centuries, but the first tonic water as we would know it today (sparkling water with quinine) dates from 1851. Erasmus Bond, a Victorian businessman and mineral water manufacturer, patented an "improved aerated tonic liquid" which was originally intended solely for its health benefits. Schweppes, already famous for their carbonated water, released their first tonic water in the 1870s and were the first large, commercial brand to sell the product.

In 2005, Charles Rolls (who had worked with Plymouth Gin in the late 20th century) and Tim Warrillow released their tonic water, Fever-Tree Premium Indian Tonic Water. This led the way for an expansion in the market. Following the recent success and the reviving fortunes of gin, the variety of tonic waters available has increased significantly, especially in Spain, where the Gin Tonica is driving innovation. In addition to an increase in the number of premium tonic waters available, more flavoured varieties have been released, too. Old favourites such as lemon or lime have been joined by new varieties such as pink peppercorn, elderflower, cherry blossom and even tomato.

Transatlantic gin | GIN STYLE

A gin that bridges the gap between classic and contemporary gins, first appearing in the late 1990s. This gin style is named after the Transatlantic (or mid-Atlantic) accent that was popular with film stars in the 1930s and 1940s; it uniquely combined the typical speaking styles from British (or British Received Pronunciation) and American English. Transatlantic gins are sometimes also known as "Cary Grant" or

SEE ALSO
Classic gin p61
Contemporary gin p65
London gin p151

"Katherine Hepburn" gins, as both of these actors had a Transatlantic accent. This style of gin has its origins firmly rooted in the tradition of London gin, but adds a twist to the classic style that is not quite as bold an innovation to make it contemporary. The first Transatlantic gin to be readily identified as such was Junipero from Anchor Distilling in San Francisco, which has been described as "a London dry gin that moved to California, then got a tan and a six-pack". Other Transatlantic gins include Rehorst Gin from Wisconsin, Big Gin from Seattle and Warner Edwards Gin from Harrington, UK.

SEE ALSO
ABV *p13*
Base spirit *p21*
Gin & Cola *p103*
Gin & Tonic *p104*
Tonic water *p226*

Uganda Waragi | BRAND

Waragi, meaning "war gin", is a gin brand owned by Uganda Breweries Ltd, part of Diageo and produced in the African country of Uganda. It is sold at 40% ABV both in bottles and 100ml (3½ fl oz) plastic sachets, similar in appearance to oversized ketchup packets. Uganda Waragi was first produced in 1965 by East Africa Distillers and uses a base spirit made from millet. It is currently Uganda's best-selling spirit brand, with around 40 percent of the market share. In its country of origin, Uganda Waragi is often drunk mixed or with a splash of lime juice. Popular mixers for using it in a long drink include Coca Cola, fruit juice and tonic water.

SEE ALSO
Gibson *p97*
Red Snapper *p188*

Umami | MIXOLOGY

One of the five tastes; the other basic tastes are sweetness, saltiness, bitterness and sourness. The somewhat savoury flavour of umami is produced by glutamic acid and naturally occurring flavour components. These are picked up by specific taste receptors all over the tongue which are particularly sensitive to it. The substance behind umami was first identified in 1866 and it was classified as a separate taste in 1908 by the Japanese scientist Kikunae Ikeda. Umami is often found in fish, mushrooms, cured meats and vegetables such as spinach, tomatoes and celery. It is also commonly identified in soy sauce and yeast extract. A good example of umami is the combination of cheese and tomato, whether that be in a pasta dish, pizza, or even a cheeseburger with ketchup. In the gin world, umami is most commonly found in cocktails such as the Gibson or Red Snapper.

SEE ALSO

Botanicals *p39*
Pot distillation *p182*
Rectification *p187*
Rotovap *p194*
Vapour distillation *p234*

Vacuum distillation | PRODUCTION

Technically, most examples of "vacuum distillation" do not take place under a true vacuum, but rather under reduced pressure. The distillation process takes place within an airtight system where the air is removed via a pump; this lowers the pressure. As the pressure decreases, the boiling points of liquids, in particular, also decrease. Most systems reduce the pressure so that alcohol boils between 20 and 30°C (68 and 86°F), as opposed to 78°C (172°F). This lower boiling point means that the alcohol and any botanicals are subject to less heat and, as such, botanicals are not cooked and are less likely to break down and release stewed flavours. Advocates of vacuum distilling proclaim that it produces a fresher and more genuine flavour. The process also enables the use of some botanicals that would burn in a traditional pot still, especially any ingredients containing large amounts of sugar. The downside of vacuum distilling is that the capital expenditure is larger relative to the size of the still and more maintenance is needed, especially for the air pumps. Vacuum-distilled gins include Sacred and Oxley. The latter gin is distilled at such a pressure that it distils at −5°C (23°F).

V

233

SEE ALSO
Botanical recipe *p36*
Botanicals *p39*
Hernö *p128*

Vanilla *VANILLA PLANIFOLIA* | BOTANICAL

A spice from the seed pod of the vanilla orchid, this is the second most expensive botanical in the world. Vanilla is native to Central America and Mexico. It also grows in the Caribbean and Madagascar. The primary commercial supply of vanilla comes from the Indian Ocean island of Madagascar, where it was introduced by the French in the mid-19th century. Before this time, Mexico was the primary producer. The French also exported vanilla orchids to the Réunion and Comoros Islands. Vanilla has a soft, sweet and creamy flavour with a smooth hint of butter and floral notes. Vanilla from Tahiti is from a different genus and has a more fruity and floral character, with hints of cherry and anise. Used sparingly in gin, vanilla pods add a smoothness to the spirit's texture, as well as a sweet creaminess. Vanilla is also a key ingredient for cream soda and the Italian liqueurs Galliano and Tuaca. Gins using vanilla as a botanical include Hernö, Zuidam Dutch Courage Gin and McQueen Mocha Gin.

SEE ALSO
Bombay Spirits Company *p33*
Botanicals *p39*
Carter head still *p50*
Greenall's *p126*
Hendrick's *p127*
Pot distillation *p182*
Vacuum distillation *p233*

Vapour distillation | PRODUCTION

Invented in the mid-19th century, vapour distillation involves placing the botanicals in a gin basket or vapour basket rather than placing them directly in the pot of the still with the alcohol, as is the case when gin is distilled by pot distillation. When the alcohol is heated, it boils and turns into vapour, which then rises through the still and passes through the perforated basket containing the botanicals. As the alcohol vapour passes over the botanicals, it extracts some of their aromas and flavours. The advantage of vapour distillation is that the

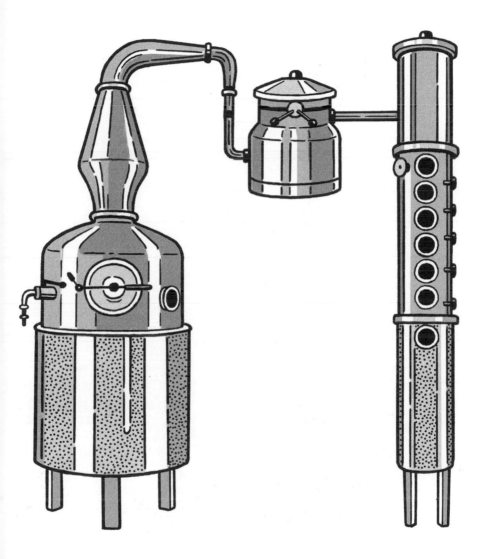

botanicals are farther away from the heat source and so stay cooler throughout the distillation process. This means that they don't start to break down or become stewed or cooked, which can negatively affect the flavour of the gin. Because of this, vapour distillation is often favoured by distillers using delicate botanicals such as fresh leaves or flowers. As the vapour passes from the base of the basket to the top, the order in which the botanicals are placed can make a significant difference to the gin's flavour, with the flavours of the botanicals placed on top being more easily extracted than those underneath. Vapour distillation is often associated with the Carter head still, a particular type of still which is used by Greenall's, Bombay Sapphire and Hendrick's.

Vesper | COCKTAIL

First mentioned in Ian Fleming's 1953 book *Casino Royale*, the Vesper is a cocktail ordered by Fleming's most famous creation, James Bond, British agent 007. The drink is a variation on a Martini and, unusually, features both vodka and gin. Ian Fleming created the drink with his friend Ivar Bryce in the early 1950s in Jamaica. It was named after a frozen rum drink that was served at sunset at another mutual friend's house; in this case, "vesper" was presumably a reference to the evening prayers. In *Casino Royale*, Bond names the cocktail after the book's leading lady.

The original ingredients of the Vesper have received a lot of attention as many have changed since the early 1950s. The Gordon's gin would have been at a stronger 47.3% ABV and the vodka would have likely been at 50% ABV. The original recipe calls for Kina Lillet, which has held the

SEE ALSO
ABV *p13*
Garnishes *p93*
Glassware *p119*
Gordon's *p120*
Ice *p135*
Lillet *p147*
Martini *p159*
Shaken/Shaking *p201*

V
237

greatest fascination for drinks researchers, as the version that Fleming used has long since disappeared; a modern alternative – Lillet Blanc – is commonly used instead, but it is less bitter.

VESPER RECIPE

90ML / 3FL OZ / GORDON'S GIN
30ML / 1FL OZ / VODKA
15ML / ½FL OZ / LILLET BLANC
LEMON TWIST, TO GARNISH

Place all the ingredients into a cocktail shaker filled with ice, shake well and strain into a cocktail glass. Garnish with a twist of lemon.

Vilnius gin | GIN STYLE

SEE ALSO
Botanicals *p39*
Coriander seed *p68*
Juniper (common) *p137*
Sweet orange *p216*

Vilnius gin, or *Vilniaus Džinas*, was a dry gin made in the city of Vilnius, Lithuania. It was protected by a Geographic Indicative Status awarded and enforced by the European Union (EU). The protection formed part of a grandfather clause when Lithuania joined the EU in 2004. In 2014, Vilnius gin lost its protected geographical status when the distillery chose not to submit a technical file to renew it. The gin has since been renamed Mr Stacher's. The gin is made at the Vilniaus Degtinė Distillery, which opened in 1907, although the gin was not produced until the 1980s. It is flavoured by the distillation of botanicals, including juniper, dill seed, coriander and orange.

Wormwood *ARTEMISIA ABSINTHIUM* | BOTANICAL

SEE ALSO
Botanical recipe *p36*
Botanicals *p39*
Dry vermouth *p80*
Red vermouth *p191*

A collective term for herbaceous plants and shrubs of the genus *Artemisia*. With reference to drinks, the main variety of interest is Grand Wormwood (*Artemisia absinthium*). This is native to Europe, Asia and North Africa. The name "wormwood" comes from the fact that the plant has been used for more than two thousand years as a worming agent and treatment for internal parasites. Wormwood is a key ingredient in a number of alcoholic drinks such as vermouth, the name of which has its origins in the German word for wormwood, *vermut*. It is also a major component of absinthe, where it is often distilled along with a variety of other botanicals. Wormwood contains thujone, a chemical that was blamed for absinthe's psychedelic properties, one of the claims that resulted in it being banned in 1915. In gin, wormwood is used as a botanical for products such as The Botanist and Elephant Gin, where it adds an aromatic, woody note.

Worshipful Company of Distillers | HISTORY

SEE ALSO
Gin Guild *p107*

Founded in 1638, the Worshipful Company of Distillers is a Livery company in the City of London. It was set up by Sir Theodore de

Mayerne, who was the physician to King Charles I, in order to regulate the distilling trade in the Cities of London and Westminster and the surrounding areas. The heraldic motto of the Company is *"Drop as Rain, Distil as Dew"*. While the Company no longer regulates the distilling trade, today it is made up of current members of the drinks industry and the descendants of members of the industry from years gone by. They organize a range of drinks-related events throughout the year, including a City debate where a current topic of the drinks industry is discussed and an annual tasting of Gold-medal-winning spirits from the International Wine and Spirits Competition. The Worshipful Company of Distillers is the parent Livery Company of the Gin Guild.

SEE ALSO

Aged gin *p15*
Botanicals *p39*
Juniper (common) *p137*
Plymouth Gin *p178*
Pot distillation *p182*
Vapour distillation *p234*
Vilnius gin *p238*

Xoriguer (Mahon) Gin | BRAND

The only dry gin that has a Geographical Indication (GI) since the lapsing of the GIs for both Plymouth in the UK and Vilnius in Lithuania. By European Union law, a gin can only be called Xoriguer Mahon Gin if it is made on the Mediterranean island of Menorca. The history of the gin goes back to 1708, when the British occupied the island before it was formally ceded to them in 1713. The natural harbour of Mahon became a major base for the British Royal Navy. The popularity of gin among the various colonial officials and military personnel in the area led to a gin distillery being set up on the island and that distillery is still open today. The gin is based on wine alcohol and is made with juniper berries and a selection of other secret botanicals. The juniper is placed directly in the pot still, while the other botanicals are placed in a botanical basket and their flavours extracted through vapour distillation. Unusually, the vapour is recycled, so it passes through the vapour basket several times, picking up more of the botanicals' aroma and flavour with every pass. The gin is made using wood-fired copper stills and, after distillation, is placed in large oak barrels. These barrels have little impact on the flavour, colour or aroma of the gin, but do allow it to breathe.

SEE ALSO

Aged gin *p15*
Booth's *p34*
Gin & Tonic *p104*
Martini *p159*
Seagram's *p198*
Single Bottle Act *p203*
Sipping gin *p207*

Yellow gin | GIN STYLE

A subcategory of aged gin, yellow gin is inspired by how gin was stored and shipped in the 19th century. At this time, gin was stored in wooden barrels or casks, rather than glass bottles or stainless steel containers. The casks would be filled at the distillery and then shipped to the public houses, where the gin would be served straight from the barrel or blended with other barrels to create a house style. Barrels were used as they were watertight, relatively durable and affordable. They could also be reused, as long as they still held liquid. Any impact that the barrel had on the flavour of the gin was incidental. Barrels were eventually replaced by glass bottles following the Single Bottle Act of 1851, which enabled distilleries to sell gin directly to consumers by the bottle. However, finished gin and the neutral spirit to make gin were still stored in barrels until after the Second World War.

In the 20th century, two gins were released that had a slight wood finishing: Booth's Finest (known as House of Lords in the United States) and Seagram's Ancient Bottle Distilled Dry Gin, released in 1939. Yellow gin was favoured by writers such as Kingsley Amis and David Embury. They were designed to be mixed as a dry gin would be, for example in Martinis and Gin & Tonics, but the effects of the wood aging would make the flavours more mellow, soft and more refined. Modern-day yellow gins include Hayman's Family Reserve and Citadelle Réserve.

SEE ALSO
Old Tom gin *p171*
Old Tom gin, Origins of *p173*

Young Tom | HISTORY

A mysterious style of gin that dates back to the mid-19th century and was possibly a stronger and more expensive version of the more famous Old Tom gin. Information on Young Tom is limited, with only a mere handful of direct references made to the style. In the 1836 *Gin Shop* in *Sketches by Boz* (a pseudonym of Charles Dickens), the writer describes large barrels in a gin shop:

"there are two side-aisles of great casks, painted green and gold, enclosed within a light brass rail and bearing such inscriptions, as 'Old Tom, 549;' 'Young Tom, 360;' 'Samson, 1421'—the figures agreeing, we presume, with 'gallons,' understood."

The Young Tom barrel was easily the smallest, which may point to the fact that it was the most valuable spirit. An 1867 advert for Tuckers Wine and Spirits Merchant at the Swan Tavern on Mile End Road, London, heralds the sale of Young Tom gin, which it describes as "much stronger than his father Old Tom". This is a reference to the stronger alcoholic strength of the Young Tom. At a time when gin was often adulterated or diluted with things other than pure spring water, the stronger the gin, the purer and the higher the perceived quality. Another reference comes from the transcript of a court case from 1903: Boord's vs. Huddart. In the case, an old gin bottle label book is given as evidence. It contains two labels: one of Old Tom, showing an old man, and the other, Young Tom, showing a young sailor.

SEE ALSO

Botanicals *p39*
Grapefruit *p124*
Lemon *p143*
Lime (Persian) *p148*

Yuzu *CITRUS X JUNOS* | BOTANICAL

A small, Japanese citrus fruit that looks somewhat like a miniature grapefruit with a bumpy rind. The fruit originated in central China and Tibet and was brought to Japan via the Korean peninsula. It has a slightly sour flavour somewhat reminiscent of a mix of lemon and lime. The flesh of the fruit is fibrous and contains seeds that are large relative to its size. Yuzu can be juiced, but the yield per fruit is low. Yuzu is a popular botanical in Japanese gin because of its close association with the country. When distilled, either the peel or the whole fruit is used.

SEE ALSO

ABV *p13*
Dry vermouth *p80*
Glassware *p119*
Ice *p135*
Navy strength gin *p167*
Shaken/Shaking *p201*

Zanzibar | COCKTAIL

First recorded in Harry Craddock's 1930 book, *The Savoy Cocktail Book*, this cocktail is essentially a shaken Vermouth Sour which nonetheless gives the gin an opportunity to shine. It is particularly suitable as a pre-dinner aperitif. Given that the gin is a small proportion of the overall drink, the final alcoholic strength of the drink is lower than many of its contemporaries; vermouth is typically only around 20% ABV. With that in mind, an intense gin, such as a navy strength gin, can showcase its flavours in this cocktail.

ZANZIBAR RECIPE

30ML / 1 FL OZ / DRY VERMOUTH
10ML / ⅓ FL OZ / NAVY STRENGTH GIN
10ML / ⅓ FL OZ / FRESH LEMON JUICE
1 PINCH OF CASTER SUGAR (OR TO TASTE)
2–3 DASHES OF ORANGE BITTERS

Place all the ingredients into a cocktail shaker filled with ice, shake well and strain into a cocktail glass.

Index

page numbers in *italic* refer to illustrations

A
....

ABV 13
aged gin *14*, 15
almond (*Prunus dulcis
    var. dulcis*) 15–16
alpine 16, *17*
anethole 16–19
angelica root (*Angelica
    archangelica*) *18*, 19
Angostura bitters 19–20
anise camphor 16–19
Aussie gin 43
Aviation 20

B
.....

base spirit 21–2
bathtub gin 22, *23*
bergamot orange (*Citrus
    bergamia*) 22–5
bitter almond (*Prunus
    dulcis var. amara*) *24*, 25
bitter lemon 26, *27*, 153
bitter orange (*Citrus ×
    aurantium*) 26–9, 174
black cardamom (*Amomum
    subulatum*) 46–9
black peppercorn (*Piper
    nigrum*) *28*, 29–30
blended gin 30, *31*
blue ginger (*Alpinia
    galanga*) 93
Bombay Spirits
    Company *32*, 33–4
Booth's 34
Borovička 35
botanical cuts 35–6
botanical recipe 36–9,
    37
botanicals *38*, 39 (*see also
    individual types*)
bramble 39–40

British juniper (*Juniperus
    communis*) 40–2, *41*
Burrough's 42–3
Bush gin 43

C
.....

Calamus (*Acorus calamus*)
    45
Campari *44*, 45–6
caraway (*Carum carvi*) 46,
    47
cardamom (*Elettaria
    cardamomum,
    Amomum subulatum*) 46–9
Carterhead still *48*, 49–50
cassia bark (*Cinnamomum
    cassia*) 50–3, *51*
Ceylon cinnamon
    (*Cinnamomum verum*)
    57
chamomile (*Chamaemelum
    nobile*) 52, 53
charge 54
cilantro (*Coriandrum
    sativum*) 54–7, *55*
cinnamon (*Cinnamomum
    verum*) 56, 57
citrus 58, *59*
citrus fruits, *see by type*
classic gin 58–61
Clover Club *60*, 61
cloves (*Syzygium
    aromaticum*) 62, *63*
cocktail ingredients, *see
    by type*
cocktails, *see by name*
cold compounded gin
    64
common gin 62–4
common juniper (*Juniperus
    communis*) 40–2, *41*, *136*,
    137–8

compounded gin 64
contemporary gin 65
contract distillers 66, 67
cordial gin 67–8
coriander 54 7, 55
coriander seed (*Coriandrum sativum*) 68, 69
cream gin 70
Crème de Genière 70–1
Crème de Violette 71–3
cubeb berries (*Piper cubeba*) 72, 73
cucumber (*Cucumis sativus*) 73–4

D

diamond method 75
Dirty Martini 75–6, 77
distillation 76 (*see also* vapour distillation)
distiller 76–9
distillery 78, 79
dry vermouth 80

E

elder (*Sambucus nigra*) 81
English lavender (*Lavandula angustifolia*) 142, 143

F

filtration 82, 83
Finsbury Gin 84, 85
fixatives 84–7
flavour profiles 86, 87 (*see also individual types*)
floral 87–8
French 75 (cocktail) 88–91, 89
French vermouth 80

fruit cups 90, 91–2
fruit gin 92

G

galangal (*Alpinia galanga*) 93
garnishes 93–4, 95
genever 94–7
Genever gin 94–7
Gibson 96, 97
Gilbey's 98
Gimlet 98–100, 99
Gin Act 1729 (UK) 100
Gin Act 1736 (UK) 101
Gin Act 1751 (UK) 101–3
Gin & Cola 102, 103–4
Gin & Tonic 104–7, 105
Gin Guild 107
gin house 106, 107–8
Gin Lane 108–10, 109
gin liqueurs 110
gin palace 111
gin renaissance 7
Gin Rickey 111–13
gin styles, *see individual styles*
Gin Tonica 112, 113–14
Ginebra San Miguel 114, 115
ginger ale 116–17
ginger wine 117
ginger (*Zingiber officinale*) 114–16
Ginniver 119
glassware 118, 119–20
Gordon's 120–3, 121
grains of paradise (*Aframomum melegueta*) 122, 123–4
grapefruit (*Citrus × paradisi*) 124–5
green cardamom (*Elettaria cardamomum*) 49

Green Chartreuse 125–6
Greenall's 126
Guinea peppers (*Aframomum melegueta*) 122, 123–4

H

Hendrick's 127
herbal gin 127–8
Hernö 128, 129
Hollands gin 131
honey 130, 131–2
hybrid gin 132–3

I

ice 134, 135
Italian vermouth 190, 191

J

Java pepper (*Piper cubeba*) 72, 73
jenever 94–7
Jenny 84, 85
juniper (common) (*Juniperus communis*) 40–2, 41, 136, 137–8
juniper-forward gin 58, 139
juniper (other species) (*Juniperus sp.*) 136, 138–9

K

kaffir lime (*Citrus hystrix*) 156
Key lime (*Citrus × aurantiifolia*) 140, 141
Kina Lillet 146, 147–8

L

The Last Word 222–5, *224*
lavender (*Lavandula
    angustifolia*) *142*, 143
lemon (*Citrus* x *limon*)
    143–4
lemongrass (*Cymbopogon
    citratus*) 144–7, *145*
licorice root (*Glycyrrhiza
    glabra*) 147
Lillet *146*, 147–8
lime (Persian) (*Citrus* x
    latifolia) 148, *149*
Lime Rickey 111–13
limonene 148–50
linalool 150
liqueurs 110 (*see also
    by name*)
London cut 151
London gin 151–3
Long Pedlar 153
louching *152*, 153–4

M

maceration 155–6
Mahon Gin, *see* Xoriguer
makrut lime (*Citrus hystrix*)
    156
Martin Miller's 156–9, *157*
Martini 75–6, *77*, *158*,
    159–60 (*see also by type*)
Martini gadgets 160–3, *161*
w (*Filipendula ulmaria*) *162*,
    163
mint (*Mentha sp.*) 164 (*see also*
    peppermint; spearmint)
mixers, *see by name*
mixology, *see by type*
myrtle (*Syzygium, Myrica,
    Backhousia sp.*) 164–5

N

Navy-strength gin *166*, 167
Negroni 168, *169*
nutmeg (*Myristica fragrans*)
    168–70

O

Old Tom gin 67, 171–3, *172*
    origins of 173–4
orange (*Citrus sinensis*) 174
orris root (*Iris 'florentina'*)
    174, *175*

P

peppermint (*Mentha* ×
    piperita) *176*, 177
Persian lime (*Citrus* x
    latifolia) 148, *149*
pinene 177–8
pink peppercorn (*Schinus
    molle*) 178, *179*
Plymouth Gin 178–81
pomelo (*Citrus maxima*)
    180, 181–2
pot distillation 182
Prohibition 183
proofing 183

Q

quininated gin *184*, 185
quinine (*Cinchona
    officinalis*) 185–6

R

Rangpur lime (*Citrus x
    limonia*) 187
rectification 187–8
Rectifiers' Club 188

Red Snapper 188–91, *189*
red vermouth *190*, 191
redistilling 187–8
rose (*Rosa sp.*) 192, *193*
rosemary (*Rosmarinus officinalis*) 192–4
rotovap 194–5
royal gin (Geneva) 195

S
.....
saffron (*Crocus sativus*) *196*, 197
sage (*Salvia officinalis*) 197–8
Sales of Spirits Act 1750 (UK) 101–3
Seagram's 198–201, *199*
Seville (*Citrus* × *aurantium*) 26–9, 174
shaddock (*Citrus maxima*) *180*, 181–2
shaken/shaking *200*, 201–2
signature botanical gin 202–3
signature serve 203
Single Bottle Act 203–4
single shot 204–7, *205*
sipping gin *206*, 207–8
sloe gin 208, *209*
soda water 208–11
sour orange (*Citrus* × *aurantium*) 26–9, 174
spearmint (*Mentha spicata*) *210*, 211–12
spicy 212
spirits, *see by name*
Spirits Duties Act 1735 (UK) 101
spontaneous emulsification *152*, 153–4
star anise (*Illicium verum*) 212–15, *213*

stirred/stirring *214*, 215
strawberry gin 215–16
sweet orange (*Citrus* × *sinensis*) 174, 216–18, *217*
sweetening the still 218

T
.....
Tahiti lime (*Citrus* x *latifolia*) 148, *149*
Tanqueray 219–21
terroir *220*, 221
test still 222, *223*
Thai ginger (*Alpinia galanga*) 93
throwing 225–6
The Last Word 222–5, *224*
tonic syrup 226
tonic water 226–8, *227*
Transatlantic gin 228–9
true cardamom (*Elettaria cardamomum*) 49
true cinnamon (*Cinnamomum verum*) 57

U
.....
Uganda Waragi *230*, 231
umami 231–2

V
....
vacuum distillation 233
vanilla (*Vanilla planifolia*) 234
vapour distillation 234–7, *235* (*see also* distillation)
Vesper *236*, 237–8
Vilniaus Džinas 238
Vilnius gin 238
Volstead Act 183

W
......
wormwood (*Artemisia absinthium*) 239
Worshipful Company of Distillers 239–40

X
.....
Xoriguer (Mahon) Gin 241

Y
....
yellow gin *242*, 243–4
Young Tom 244
yuzu (*Citrus junos*) 245

Z
.....
Zanzibar *246*, 247

Acknowledgments

The author would like to thank the following people for their help with this book: The Gin Archive, Nicholas Cook of The Gin Guild, Aaron J Knoll, Clayton and Ali Hartley, Queenie, Tas, Joe Barber, Bernadette Pamplin, Cherry Constable, Dr Anne Brock, Gin Miller, Julia Nourney, Veronika Karlova, Jimmy Young, Bobby Evans, Rosie the Bear, Ian Hart, Hilary Whitney, Olivier and Julia Ward, Sarah Mitchell, Adam Smithson, Unkie Des, Sam Carter, Stephen Gould, Helen Cheshire, Jon Hillgren, The Hayman Family, Sean Harrison, Davey Wonder, Phil Duff, Jared Brown and Anistatia Miller, Camper, Jake Burger esq., Geraldine Coates, Tommy and Michael Haughton, Dave Hughes, Alice Lascelles, Seb Hamilton-Mudge, Charlie Maxwell, Henrik Hammer, Dan Szor, Eric Zandona, Bill Owens, Dame Keli Rivers, Natasha Bahrami, Michael Vachon, Ben Ellefsen, Alan Stibbe, Martin Miller, Tempus Fugit, The Bitter Truth, The Diageo Archive, David W Smith and JP Smith.

Joe Cottington, Jonathan Christie, Polly Poulter, Matthew Grindon and Megan Brown at Octopus; Joanna Smith and Corinne Masciocchi for their editorial assistance; MFE Editorial Services for the index; Stuart Patience for his fantastic illustrations.

Finally a special thanks to Sara Smith without whom the book would not be possible.

An Hachette UK Company

www.hachette.co.uk

First published in Great Britain in 2018 by Mitchell Beazley,
a division of Octopus Publishing Group Ltd
Carmelite House
50 Victoria Embankment
London EC4Y 0DZ
www.octopusbooks.co.uk
www.octopusbooksusa.com

255

Distributed in the US by
Hachette Book Group
1290 Avenue of the Americas
4th and 5th Floors
New York, NY 10104

Distributed in Canada by
Canadian Manda Group
664 Annette St.
Toronto, Ontario, Canada M6S 2C8

ISBN 9781784723989

A CIP catalogue record for this book is available from the British Library.

Printed and bound in China

10 9 8 7 6 5 4 3 2 1

Commissioning Editor: Joe Cottington
Senior Editor: Pollyanna Poulter
Copy Editor: Joanna Smith
Creative Director: Jonathan Christie
Illustrator: Stuart Patience
Production Controller: Dasha Miller

About the author

David T. Smith is an internationally renowned gin expert, judge and author. He chairs judging panels for the American Distilling Institute and the International Wine and Spirits Competition, as well as the Gin Masters competition. Winner of the 2016 Think Gin award for best communicator, David runs workshops on the art of gin distilling as well as the drinks website Summer Fruit Cup.